The New Testament Church
then and now

by LeRoy Lawson

STANDARD PUBLISHING
Cincinnati, Ohio   88585

Library of Congress Cataloging in Publication Data

Lawson, E. LeRoy, 1938-
  The New Testament church, then and now

    1. Church. 2. Church history—Primitive and early
church, ca. 30-600. I. Title.
BV600.2.L35   262   81-50631
ISBN 0-87239-443-3   AACR2

Except where otherwise specified, Scripture quotations are from the *Revised Standard Version* of the Bible.

Contents

The Most Important Church in the World

I am the minister of the most important church in the world.
This fact has only slowly dawned on me. It was Dr. Charles
Allen, of the twelve-thousand-member First Methodist Church
at Houston, Texas, who first brought it to my attention. I attended a convention in which he addressed a group of ministers, and in the midst of his message he casually said some
things about the church that to him was the most important
church in the world. I thought he was going to speak about his
impressive Houston church, the biggest in his denomination.
Instead, he told us about a little frame church building nestled
in the hills where, among the humble members of that congregation, he first met Christ. For Allen, there could never be a
more important church.

I thought immediately of the modest church I attended in
Tillamook, Oregon. There was nothing exceptional about that
building either, except that it seemed to leak profusely during
the interminable rains in that coast town. But what a church!
There I met the Lord and grew up in the midst of some of the
tallest spiritual giants I have ever known. I have often won-
dered what my life would have been without the powerful influence of that church. I have served great congregations in my
ministry, but for me that will always seem the most important
church in the world—for there I met Christ.

Yet having said that about my home church, I hasten to add that the church I now serve seems the most important. Here each week men and women are responding to Christ's invitation to follow Him; before my eyes they are growing into bigger and better persons. The Spirit of the living God is at work here, daily reminding me that there is no more significant work in the world than the ministry of the church and, for me now, no more important place to serve. The rewards just keep multiplying. I could tell you about hundreds of persons whose lives have been permanently transformed—mechanics, machinists, housewives, carpenters, assembly line workers, doctors, businessmen, teachers, nurses, farmers, and many, many more— for whom *this* is the most important church in the world.

This has always been true of the church. To read through the New Testament is to be struck anew with the writers' conviction that there is no more imperative task one can perform than to help others come to know Jesus as Lord, and no more significant organization than the church to accomplish that assignment. In this study book, we shall be rereading the New Testament to learn what the earliest churches looked like. We want to do that, because our churches today should imitate, as much as possible, what they looked like in the beginning. To be genuine churches, today's congregations must demonstrate the same essential qualities that characterized the church ideal from the beginning.

As we begin the study, let me remind you that your church is as important to you as the one I am now serving and the one that brought me up in Christ are to me. Here are some of the reasons:

1) *You meet the Lord in your church.* "Where two or three are gathered in my name, there am I in the midst of them," Jesus said (Matthew 18:20). The regular meetings of your congregation are centered on Christ. Here you study about Him in the Bible, you meet at His table, you pray in His name, you try to grow up to be like Him, and you work to introduce others to Him. It is only "through the church [that] the manifold wisdom of God might now be made known" (Ephesians 3:10). The most important assignment in the world—that of saving lives—has not been given to government or political parties or educational institutions, but to the church—this church.

I was having breakfast with a friend of mine in Portland,

Oregon, when another of his friends joined us. As we became acquainted, we talked rather aimlessly about nothing in particular until he learned that I am preacher. The conversation shifted immediately because he wanted to talk about God. That happens quite a bit to me, because the world is full of people who want to talk about God. They are interested in Him, but don't see much of Him in the world at large. That's what makes Christians and their churches so important. They are indeed lights in a dark world, cities set upon a hill. They are the way by which people can find God.

2) *You become excited about life here.* It has become a cliche of our day that most persons live lives of quiet desperation. They are bored and boring. I didn't know that as a young person, because I belonged to that important church I was telling you about. The people I knew seemed charged with energy; they were happy, caring, hardworking Christians for whom each new day held another opportunity to serve the Lord. Our quiet little community never seemed quiet to me; there was too much going on in our church for me ever to be bored. My best friends were in the church, my best times were with church people. And they were the ones who cared most about me. Thanks to them, life was—and has always been—exciting for me.

Not too long ago I visited some old friends from another church. These are people I have known for twenty years or more. Talk about excited! In the years we have been apart, Christ has touched them in new ways and Christ has led them into a deepened and broadened experience with Him. Their health is better than it has ever been, many of their personal problems have dissolved, and new enthusiasm has charged them with energy they have never had before. They sounded like the effervescent apostle Paul who found cause to rejoice in the Lord in every circumstance (Philippians 4). There was nothing dull or routine about his Christian life—or the lives of my friends.

Some churches, unfortunately, seem rather unexciting. Perhaps I could not have written this book if I had been part of such congregations. My experience has been the opposite. The churches I have been a part of have been alive and vigorous bodies. But I did preach for one that nearly broke my heart. I wasn't with the group very long, but long enough to diagnose the difficulty. It had once been a vigorous church, but that was in the past, a past which the current leaders remembered as the

Golden Age. That Golden Age killed the present; the leaders revered their past, defeated any suggestion of a program that was different from what they had always done. They walked by fear of change rather than by faith in God. There was no excitement there.

Most of the churches I have known have heeded Paul's admonition to the Roman Christians:

> Let love be genuine; hate what is evil, hold fast to what is good; love one another with brotherly affection; outdo one another in showing honor. Never flag in zeal, be *aglow* with the Spirit, serve the Lord (Romans 12:9-11).*

Church life isn't just a matter of hard work and earnest service; it's a matter of glowing. God comes to us in His Spirit and we receive Him. We then enter into partnership with Him in an adventure without parallel.

Let me use Bob Wetzel as an example. We worked together as fellow professors for several years. In those days we both prayed about our futures and what specific assignment God would have for us. That prayer was answered for both of us. Mine took me back to the pastoral ministry; his to mission work in England. At our first reunion after he had answered the call to England and before leaving for the field, I saw what had happened to him. His face was aglow; he was animated with new energy. We met at a convention. He had no room, so I invited him to stay with me in mine—provided he would let me get some sleep, I added. He promised he would and moved in, but we didn't sleep much. I didn't expect to. The glow was too bright.

There is something invigorating about working with such people. You can understand why I enjoy the ministry so much. The congregation I serve is filled with glowing Christians. There is a joy among us. We all believe in what we are doing, and are doing it with all our might. We are excited.

3) *You learn to care about others here.* Several chapters of this study book will emphasize the caring ministry of the church. That is deliberate, to impress us with the fact that a church that doesn't care is scarcely a church.

An old friend of mine taught me this fact about Christianity. He's a college mate who was once very active in his Christian life, but who became disenchanted through the years and is not in church at all now. I expect him back, but it'll be a while. The reason I expect him back is that he is a very sensitive man, as kind a person as I know. Not having been a part of a church for several years now, he has been brooding about the best way to meet the needs of the world's people. The last time we were together he said, "You know, there really is no other caring community besides the church." He's right. The church exists because it cares. It has no other reason to be.

But caring for others is not the natural impulse of our world. It is the opposite of the "me first" philosophy so popular now. That's why I said that we *learn* to care in the church. We have to be taught. Sometimes we'll resist, because Christ's teachings run so counter to much that we learn in public schools and all of the media. I'll not say more about this now, because I'll be saying so much more later.

4) *You grow into Christlikeness here.* One of my reasons for being so positive about Christians is that I have been watching them for many years now, and I like the progress I see. Oh yes, there are many disappointments. It is as easy to find hypocrites in the church as in any other human group. And some Christian failures are so spectacular in their fall that they bring dishonor to all of Christianity. But they are not the whole story. They are not even most of the story. Many of my Christian brothers and sisters have not only grown older through the years, but they have grown better. This is what makes our reunions so much fun. We compare notes about what improvements God has made in our lives since we were together last—and some of us needed much improving.

In recent years I have become a more enthusiastic preacher than I was as a young man. I speak with more conviction, because I have lived long enough now to see the evidence. I have seen many persons improve and many others deteriorate. The difference is in what they have allowed the Spirit of God to do with them through the years. As a result, in my preaching I can confidently promise people, "If you'll stick with this church long enough, if you'll immerse yourself in the Word of God, if you'll reach out to others in love and learn to forgive and to care, and if you'll take ahold of the hand of God and rest in His embrace, I promise you God will make you better!" That's a fact.

Paul urges us in Ephesians to "grow up in every way into

Christ." The secret of Christian growth is found in the model we are to imitate. If we set out to become like him, we'll improve. And we don't have to do it alone, either. We have the help of the Holy Spirit and the assistance of other Christians. We can't lose.

5) *You prepare for the future here.* Each year we survive together on this planet seems a little more tense than the year before. Anxiety rules everywhere. We spend multiplying billions for defense, knowing all the time that the military can provide no final defense against international insanity. Then the environmentalists tell us we are destroying our natural resources, while futurologists predict that too many people and too little fresh air and water could bring human life to an abrupt conclusion. People are frankly scared.

Not everybody is frightened, however. Christians enjoy a sense of security even in the midst of these terrifying predictions. They know the Bible prophesies that the world will come to an end, perhaps any day now. Like the earliest Christians they anticipate the return of Christ and the wrapping up of human history. Yet they look forward with faith and not with fear. They have already accepted Christ as Lord of their lives; they acknowledge Him also as Lord of history. Since they belong to Him, they have no cause to fear the future. The worst that could happen to them on earth is that they would be killed. But death has no more sting, since Christ has been proved Lord of life *and* death.

So when Christians meet regularly, they can genuinely rejoice, even in tumultuous times like these.

Much more could be said about the importance of the church—your church—today, but these five reasons should be enough to encourage you to enter this study of the church's beginnings with me. By the way, you may not want to study these chapters in the order I have given them to you. I had a plan in mind, of course, but my plan may not meet your needs. So start anywhere and proceed according to your interests. You will want to read the Scriptures given with the chapter titles. Without having read the Biblical text, you may have some difficulty following my reasoning.

Another word. You'll notice I am not bashful about my opinions. You may disagree with me freely—in fact, I'll be surprised if you don't. It doesn't matter that you and I have different opinions. What matters is that we both are honestly trying to help our churches fulfill their divine mission. To do so, we need to take a hard look at what churches were like in the beginning. That is the purpose of this book.

---

*Here and throughout this book, the author has italicized portions of the Scripture quotations for emphasis.

CHAPTER ONE

Where the Church Came From

(Acts 2)

Some of my colleagues question my judgment in attempting to write this little study book on the New Testament church. In fact, a few of them have given me up as hopelessly old-fashioned because I still cling to an organization that they delight in describing as an irrelevant monument to past glory. "There are many other groups you can belong to," they assure me, "that are meeting the needs of today's world far better than the church does—why do you bother with it when you could be doing something valuable with your life?"

It's not an easy question. You can explain the church's worship and be told that it is possible to worship alone. You can boast of the church's social services, but your antagonist will quickly point to the Red Cross and governmental welfare agencies and many other organizations whose social services may be more effective than the church's. You can testify of the peace of mind and the psychological stability you have achieved in the church, only to hear about what marvelous things psychiatry and mutual help groups are accomplishing.

How does one begin, then, to explain the continuing importance of the church? The best way is to start with where the church came from. We shall see three important sources of the New Testament church.

Perhaps I can best approach the subject indirectly. At our

house we have a desk that is extremely valuable to us. My father built it for his mother when he was in high school. It is a polished mahogany beauty that adorns any room in which it is placed. I have seen other desks somewhat like it and know them to be worth more than $500 at today's prices. But we wouldn't accept $500,000 for our desk, because my father made it. It may look like other desks, but there is not another one like it. It is my father's handiwork.

Similarly, the church may superficially resemble other organizations, but nothing else is quite like it—because it came from our Father. THE CHURCH WAS CONCEIVED IN THE MIND OF GOD. Lodges and clubs cannot compare. I know about them, because I have belonged to both. I joined one lodge after having been assured that it was based on Christian principles. As a member I did see some Christian influence upon the rituals and I enjoyed the comradeship, but I quit shortly, not because I am opposed to lodges but because this organization wasn't quite the same as the one my Father made. I would have to say the same thing about civic clubs. They are worthwhile service agencies, no doubt. I have belonged, paid my dues and done my duties. But the clubs can never come first in my life because they are not the same as what my Father made.

Thus the first answer to our question, "Where did the church come from?" is this: It was conceived in the mind of God.

The Pentecost events were God's doing—of that Peter was certain. Listen to him:

And in the last days it shall be, *God* declares . . . (Acts 2:17).

Men of Israel, hear these words: Jesus of Nazareth, a man attested to you *by God* with mighty works and wonders and signs which *God* did through him in your midst . . . (v. 22).

. . . this Jesus, delivered up *according to the definite plan and foreknowledge of God* . . . (23).

But *God* raised him up . . . (24).

. . . knowing that *God* had sworn with an oath to him that he would set one of his descendants upon his throne . . . (30).

This Jesus *God* raised up . . . (32).

Let all the house of Israel therefore know assuredly that *God* has made him both Lord and Christ, this Jesus whom you crucified (36).

The life of Christ, His death and resurrection, the miraculous events of Pentecost (see 2:1-4), and the startling miracle of

13

communication (2:5-11) can all be explained, Peter proclaims to his audience, as the working of God in their midst. For centuries, as far back as the prophets and King David, God has had something in mind. He has now fufilled His dream. He has made Jesus Lord and Christ.

Paul, writing much later, traces God's purpose even further back:

> Of this gospel I was made a minister according to the gift of God's grace which was given me by the working of his power. To me, though I am the very least of all the saints, this grace was given, to preach to the Gentiles the unsearchable riches of Christ, and to make all men see *what is the plan of the mystery* hidden for ages in God who created all things; that *through the church* the manifold wisdom of God might be made known to the principalities and powers in the heavenly places. *This was according to the eternal purpose which he has realized in Christ Jesus our Lord* . . . (Ephesians 3:7-11; see also Colossians 1:15-20).

Both Peter and Paul were confident that God does not act capriciously. What they had observed in the life of Christ, what Peter experienced on the Day of Pentecost, the subsequent response of the 3,000 souls and the continuing growth of the church through their ministries and those of others all derived from the eternal purpose of God. The church did not spring into being as the brainchild of men; it came from the mind of God.

That is what makes the church so vital. God did not choose to unveil his "manifold wisdom" through any government, because all governments, even that of the mighty Roman empire or the United States of America, flourish and then pass away. He could not call upon his myriads of angels to announce this wisdom. We would not listen to them. He could not even entrust it solely to His Son, for Jesus lived in limited time and space; the enfleshed Word had to become present in all times and places. Thus the Word that had become flesh and dwelt among us was transmitted to the church, that in every age the church might broadcast God's message.

On Pentecost Peter announced the way by which men could come into an eternal relationship with God through the grace of Jesus Christ. As recipients of this grace they were received into the fellowship of Christ's body. Those who accepted Peter's instructions were baptized, and "there were added that day about three thousand souls" (2:41). Added to what? The following verses make it clear that they were added to the Lord and to one another. They became the church.

It was all conceived in the mind of God. That is the first source.

The second is God's historical people. The church did not suddenly appear out of nowhere. *Its roots were deep in the people of Israel.*

I had been a Christian for many years before the truth suddenly struck me that I, who cannot trace my blood lineage back many generations, have no such ignorance about my religious heritage. My roots are in ancient Judaism. I can trace the line of my religious ancestors back through the reformation, through the preceding centuries of Roman Catholicism, through the developmental days of the apostolic church, to Christ; then through Christ back through the varied careers of the Jews and ancient Hebrews to the patriarchs themselves. The God of Abraham, Isaac, and Jacob is my God:

> Go from your country and your kindred and your father's house to the land that I will show you. And I will make of you a great nation, and I will bless you, and make your name great, so that you will be a blessing. I will bless those who bless you, and him who curses you I will curse; and *by you all the families of the earth shall bless themselves* (Genesis 12:1-3).

That final promise to Abram was fulfilled centuries later when Christ opened the membership in the family of God to those who were not necessarily blood descendants of Abram, but were nonetheless his spiritual heirs (see Galatians 3:6-9). It was through Christ that I, who have no Hebrew blood in me, could claim to be a member of the family of God, could call Abraham's God my God. In the nation of Israel God's promise to Abraham was transmitted from age to age as God prepared for the right moment:

> But when the time had fully come, God sent forth his Son, born of woman, born under the law, to redeem those who were under the law, *so that we might receive adoption as sons* (Galatians 4:4, 5).

Before the advent of Christ, Israel was distinctive among the

15

world's nations for a high concept of God and a consequent high moral standard. Israel was not interested in speculative theology or religious doctrines. Unlike the philosophical Greeks, the people of Israel lived their religion rather than speculated about it. They believed God was at work among them, directing their nation, fulfilling His plans. They might obey Him or disappoint Him, praise or blaspheme Him, but He was still their God and they were His people.

Through their failures and heartaches, they remained God's people. Their priests taught them, their prophets warned them, and their kings led them. Through everything they could look backward to the great events when God was obviously directing them (the exodus, the conquering of Canaan) and forward to the day when He would send the promised one, their Messiah, to rescue them from their enemies. Their prophet Jeremiah most eloquently spoke of that later day, when the covenant God had established with Moses would be succeeded by a better covenant, forming a new union between God and His people:

> Behold, the days are coming, says the Lord, when I will make a new covenant with the house of Israel and the house of Judah, not like the covenant which I made with their fathers when I took them by the hand to bring them out of the land of Egypt, my covenant which they broke, though I was their husband, says the Lord. But this is the covenant which I will make with the house of Israel after those days, says the Lord: I will put my law within them, and I will write it upon their hearts; and I will be their God, and they shall be my people. And no longer shall each man teach his neighbor and each his brother, saying 'Know the Lord,' for they shall all know me, from the least of them to the greatest, says the Lord; for I will forgive their iniquity, and I will remember their sin no more (Jeremiah 31:31-34).

God has something better in mind, Jeremiah promises. One day His people will be not only blood descendants of Abraham, but will be those who in their hearts want to be His people. God will write a new agreement. It was to this that Jesus referred on His last night when, in blessing the wine, He said, "This cup is the new covenant in my blood" (1 Corinthians 11:25). The term *new covenant* has meaning for us, however, only because of the earlier ones God established with His historical people. So rather than disdain the Old Testament as an outdated chronicle of an ancient people, we cherish it as the record of God at work, accomplishing His purposes and preparing for today's church through His people of yesterday.

On Pentecost the right moment to begin the New Covenant group had come. God gathered a new people, a new family, and brought it into being that day. God called the members of the community through the preaching of the gospel. Those who heard Peter preach responded in faith and repentance, being baptized into the name of the Messiah. Then they continued steadfastly together. They became the church.

The third source of the church was Christ himself and His intimate followers. They modeled the actual life of the *New Covenant church for the earliest Christians and for us*. There was no church when Christ was personally with the disciples, of course, but they were the prototype of the church. In a sense it all began with Jesus and His friends, living together, growing together, ministering to others. It might not be stretching the truth to call the church the "Friends of Jesus" today.

Christ defined the nature of their fellowship. He had called them and they followed Him as apprentices of a master. They were not separatists from society, like some of the religious sects of their day, but active participants with their contemporaries, reaching out in teaching, preaching, healing and, when necessary, correcting.

With His disciples Jesus laid the foundation for the church (see Ephesians 2:20). They learned the lessons He taught them, were awed by the power He commanded over man and nature, and were held by the love He steadfastly offered them. They required a resurrection before they were fully convinced of His uniqueness, but when they saw Him alive again and then received His promised Spirit, Jesus' former students began boldly to announce the good news about Him and laid claim to be the new people of God. They not only taught what they had heard Him teach but they began to do what they had seen Him do. They called others in His name to His loving fellowship; they urged repentance for forgiveness of sin because of the kingdom, just as He had done.

They realized that God had sent Christ so that men could see and know His will and purposes in the flesh. They further grasped the fact that as Christ had been the one in whom the love of God had been experienced, now His continuing body the church must be the physical embodiment of God's love on earth. The church is the purpose of God enfleshed, the incarnate Lord still embodied, serving and saving the lost.

Men do not fall in love with and devote themselves to God's purposes in the abstract. That is why Christ had to come, so that men and women could actually observe the purpose of God enacted, could see and hear and touch and believe in a Person, not an abstract ideal. Christ is the one in whom we meet the love of God on our level. He came that we might behold, and He left behind a church in which subsequent generations could experience the love of God. Therefore we Christians must live, look, sound and serve like Christ. Our model is the life of Jesus and His disciples. Jesus was the center of the disciples' band; they studied His teachings, ate meals with Him, loved and sacrificed for one another at His direction, reached out beyond themselves to others in need. What they did then, we do now. The privilege of the church is to relive the life of Christ and His disciples.

At the beginning, the leaders of the church were the same disciples who had been with Christ. Peter could boldly affirm on Pentecost, "We know that these things are true, because we were there when they happened. We know that God has raised Jesus from the dead—we have seen Him. Therefore let the whole nation of Israel know for a fact that God has made him both Lord and Christ, this Jesus whom you crucified." It was not so much a statement as a challenge: "Now what are you going to do about it? You now know what God was doing in Jesus. You also know what you did to Jesus. We are giving you this opportunity to believe in Him, to repent and turn toward Him, and be baptized in His name. If you will do these things, then forgiveness of your sins and the gift of the Holy Spirit are yours."

Not all responded, of course, but three thousand of them did. Immediately these new members of the church began to meet together. They knew what to do because their leaders, the apostles, could guide them, having been with Jesus and instructed by Him. They also had the entire heritage of Israel to draw upon. Furthermore, they believed that what was happening, and the church that was forming, had been conceived in the mind of God.

For Further Consideration

1. What makes the church important today—to you personally and to society in general?
2. How does the church differ from other organizations like lodges or service clubs?
3. What eternal purpose did God fulfill in Christ?
4. What is the relationship between the church and the ancient nation of Israel?
5. How did the Israelites differ from the Greeks?
6. How did the New Covenant differ from the Old?
7. In what way can it be said that the church began with Jesus and His disciples?
8. This chapter contains a definition of the church. What is it? Can you improve upon it?

CHAPTER TWO

Getting Into the Church:
Faith and Repentance

(Acts 2:29-42)

In the beginning there was no difference between "being saved" and being a member of the church. When Peter had completed his Pentecost sermon, his audience was convinced that he was telling the truth about Jesus Christ and their implication in His crucifixion. "They were cut to the heart," the Scripture says, and they knew that they had to do something to get right with God again. But what should they do? How could they undo the damage already done to Jesus? If what Peter said about God making Jesus the Lord and Christ were a fact, what would become of them if they did not make some sort of restitution? "Brethren, what shall we do?"

Peter's answer is straightforward: "Repent, and be baptized . . ." Inwardly and outwardly you must evidence a turning toward God. To repent is to be sorry for your participation in rejecting and slaying the promised one of God, sorry enough to change your mind and actions toward God and physically dramatize that change in baptism. Only if they united with the One they had rejected could God forgive them. Otherwise they were all like men in chains, condemned to death. Having killed the forgiver of sins, they were now without hope.

They need not despair, however. In addition to Peter's commands he offers two incredible promises: forgiveness of their sins and the gift of the Holy Spirit.

There is urgency in Peter's preaching as he further exhorts them to rescue themselves from their corrupt society. He speaks so persuasively that "there were added that day about three thousand souls." They were baptized in the name of Jesus Christ, thereby identifying with Him and His. From that moment "they devoted themselves to the apostles' teaching and fellowship, to the breaking of bread and the prayers." They had been saved.

To say that they had been saved is not to mean only that their eternal destiny had been fixed. In the New Testament, this term does not have a strictly otherworld application. To be saved is to find wholeness, completeness. It is both to be rescued from the eternal consequences of sin and to participate in Christ's victory over sin and Satan daily. To be saved is to become a member of Christ's victorious team.

Salvation therefore is not strictly between God and the individual believer. It involves God, myself, and other believers. My personal experience of God is unavoidably bound up in my relation with other persons,

> He who does not love his brother whom he has seen, cannot love God whom he has not seen. And this commandment we have from him, that he who loves God should love his brother also (1 John 4:20, 21).

Pentecost's converts, in turning toward God (repenting) and being baptized into Christ were added to one another as they were added to the Lord. They were forming the church.

By examining the accounts of the conversions recorded in Acts we find that the terms of salvation and the terms for "joining the church" are identical. Believers were not "saved" and then at some later time given an opportunity to become a member of a church. They were saved by Christ, baptized into Christ, united with Christ's body. Those who believed the gospel message and responded according to the apostles' instructions were considered members. Let's look at these examples:

Acts 3:19 "Repent therefore, and turn again, that your sins may be blotted out, that times of refreshing may come from the presence of the Lord . . ." Peter's defense of his and John's healing of the lame man includes this appeal to his opponents to turn toward the Lord because "there is salvation in no one else, for there is no other name

21

under heaven given among men by which we must be saved" (4:12). It is obvious that repentance, a deliberate turning toward Christ, is an essential for salvation.

Acts 4:32 "Now the company of those who believed were of one heart and soul, and no one said that any of the things which he possessed was his own, but they had everything in common." Here, as in Acts 2:44, 45, "the company of those who believe" were functioning as a church, taking care of each other's material needs as well as encouraging one another in faith. There is no doubt that "belief" is essential to salvation and to church membership.

Acts 4:4 "But many of those who heard the word believed; and the number of the men came to about five thousand." Belief is again the essential.

Acts 8:12 "But when they believed Philip as he preached good news about the kingdom of God and the name of Jesus Christ, they were baptized, both men and women." Baptism following belief is assumed to be part of the conversion process.

Acts 8:13 "Even Simon himself believed, and after being baptized he continued with Philip." Again baptism and belief are joined and the new convert becomes part of the company of believers.

Acts 8:36-38 "See, here is water! What is to prevent my being baptized?" Philip has been teaching the Ethiopian eunuch that the passage he was studying in Isaiah 53 is about Jesus Christ; beginning with that passage he preaches the gospel of Christ to him. The eunuch obviously believes Philip and asks for baptism, which Philip must have already explained to him.

Acts 9, 22, 26 These three chapters contain the narratives of Paul's conversion. Because of the miraculous events accompanying Christ's challenge to Saul on the Damascus road, readers sometimes concentrate on the extraordinary elements in the story instead of the more common aspects which Saul's conversion shares with the other Acts accounts. Not everyone is struck blind, nor hears a voice out of Heaven, when the Lord deals with him, but every repentant sinner has to ask, "What shall I do, Lord?" And the answer is the same to all. All must be obedient to the Lord's instructions. We note in 9:18 that after Paul has been instructed by Ananias, "he rose and was baptized . . ." In 22:16 Ananias asks Saul, "And now why do you wait? Rise and be baptized, and wash away your sins, calling on his name." In spite of his miraculous confrontation with Christ, Saul was not given special treatment. Like all other Christians he had to wash his sins away in the waters of baptism and call on the name of the only one who could cleanse him.

Acts 10:43   In Peter's address to the household of Cornelius, a non-Jewish believer in God, Peter asserts that to Christ "all the prophets bear witness that every one who believes in him receives forgiveness of sins through his name." Here forgiveness is joined with belief. In the 47th verse, Peter asks, "Can any one forbid water for baptizing these people who have received the Holy Spirit just as we have?" Then "he commanded them to be baptized in the name of Jesus Christ." In this experience the gospel jumps the cultural barrier between Jew and Gentile. We find the same four elements that we find in the Pentecost account in Acts 2: belief in Jesus Christ, baptism in the name of Jesus Christ, the forgiveness of sins, and the outpouring of the Holy Spirit.

Acts 16:14, 15   When the Lord opens Lydia's heart "to give heed to what was said by Paul," she then is "baptized, with her household." Having heard the gospel claims, she obviously believes them and obeys the apostolic instruction to be baptized. She then invites Paul and his companions to stay in her home, thus becoming a very helpful member of the church at Philippi.

Acts 16:30-33   The Philippian jailer has a similar experience. When he asks, "Men, what must I do to be saved?" Paul and Silas answer, "Believe in the Lord Jesus, and you will be saved, you and your household." The passage continues, noting that Paul and Silas spoke the word of the Lord to him and to all who were in his house, "and he took them the same hour of the night, and washed their wounds, and he was baptized at once, with all his family." He believed . . . and was baptized.

Acts 18   At Corinth, Crispus, the ruler of the synagogue "believed in the Lord, together with all his household; and many of the Corinthians hearing Paul believed and were baptized."

Acts 19:5   In this extraordinary passage, Paul found some believers at Ephesus who had been baptized into John's baptism and had not received the Holy Spirit. Paul instructed them further and they were baptized anew, this time in the name of the Lord Jesus. Then he laid hands on them and they received the Holy Spirit in a marvelous manner, speaking in tongues and prophesying, the Lord in this manner validating the name of Jesus.

What have we learned from these conversion accounts? Although we may not be able to solve all the theological disputes about the various elements of conversion, it is quite clear the writer of Acts assumes that a saving faith includes belief in Jesus of Nazareth as the Messiah, repentance (a turning toward

God in Christ and away from sin's domain), and baptism in His name. These things man can perform. Also involved are two promises that only God can perform: to forgive the sins of the penitent believer and to empower him to live for Him through the gift of the Holy Spirit. These elements—faith, repentance, baptism, forgiveness of sins and the gift of the Holy Spirit—are not treated in a ritualistic or formulated manner. Sometimes one element is stressed, sometimes another. The accumulation of the evidence, however, is that saving faith in the Lord Jesus will naturally be accompanied by a changed heart and a desire to express that change in baptism. No distinction is found in these chapters (or elsewhere in the New Testament) between being "in Christ" and being a part of the church. Those who believed were a company; that company is called the church.

We need to look a little more closely at each of these elements.

Faith

The most popular name for Christians in the New Testament is *believers*. Theirs was not the vague, contentless faith in faith that characterizes much modern religiosity; rather it was belief in God and His specific saving acts in Christ Jesus. Every living person needs to believe in something, of course. As Leo Tolstoy has said,

> If a man lives, he believes in something. If he did not believe that there was something to live for, he would not live. If he does not see and understand the unreality of the finite, he believes in the finite; if he sees the unreality, he must believe in the infinite. Without faith it is impossible to live.

So to call a person a believer today does not mean much. For this reason it is good that the term *Christian* early replaced the less definitive *believer* as our name, although belief in Christ is assumed in every Christian. Alexander Campbell, answering the question, "Who is a Christian?" underscored the importance of faith by defining a Christian as

> every one that believes in his heart that Jesus of Nazareth is the Messiah, the Son of God; repents of his sins, and obeys Him in all things according to his measure of knowledge of His will . . .

The content of the Christian's faith is spelled out in these Scriptures:

Acts 2:36 "Let all the house of Israel therefore know assuredly that *God has made him both Lord and Christ,* this Jesus whom you crucified."

Romans 10:9 ". . . if you confess with your lips that *Jesus is Lord* and believe in your heart that *God raised him from the dead,* you will be saved."

1 Corinthians 15:1-6 ". . . the gospel, which you received, in which you stand, by which you are saved, . . . that *Christ died for our sins in accordance with the scriptures,* that *he was buried,* that *he was raised on the third day* in accordance with the scriptures, and that he appeared to Cephas, then to the twelve. Then he appeared to more than five hundred brethren at one time, most of whom are still alive, though some have fallen asleep."

John 20:30, 31 "Now Jesus did many other signs in the presence of the disciples, which are not written in this book; but these are written that you may believe that Jesus is the Christ, the Son of God, and that believing you may have life in his name."

It is obvious that the New Testament term *believers* has a definite content. Christians believe in Jesus as the Christ; they accept Him as the Son of God and the source of their salvation. First-century Christians lived in a religious era like our own, with gods of all description being worshiped by their devotees. Members of each religion claimed to have faith. Christians were distinctive in the content of their faith. They believed that Christ was the revelation of all of God that mankind can understand and of all of man that we can become. He came as Son of God and Son of Man; God has made Him the one before whom every knee should bow. We do not have faith in faith, therefore; our faith is in Jesus of Nazareth, named the Christ by God, He who lived and died "that whoever believes in him should not perish but have eternal life" (John 3:16), He whom God raised from the dead as a sign that all who are in Him should likewise live.

Christian faith is more than mental assent to these facts about Jesus, however. Hebrews 11:6 states that "whoever would draw near to God must believe that he exists and that he rewards those who seek him." It is one thing to believe in the existence of God; it is quite another to so believe that you place your confidence, your trust, entirely in Him. "We walk by faith, not by sight" is Paul's way of expressing this trust (2 Corinthians

5:7). To restrict faith to an intellectual assent to facts is to court a dull, academic religion; to walk by faith is to adventure with God. The New Testament uses a phrase that does not occur in secular Greek or in the Greek Old Testament (Septuagint). It says that we *believe in* Christ; it assumes mental assent to the facts concerning Jesus' life and death and resurrection, but it goes beyond assent to trust in Him as Savior. When Peter and the apostles answered the high priest in Jerusalem, "We must obey God rather than men" (Acts 5:29), they were trusting the God who acted in Christ to take care of those who obey Him.

These two aspects of faith, content and trust, are illustrated repeatedly in the major storms that attack our country. In almost every instance, the national weather service issues warnings to residents in an area that expects a tornado touchdown or a hurricane, or whatever. After the storm, when the dead are being counted, the survivors report that some who perished did so because "they didn't believe it would be as severe as the advance warning indicated." They heard the message, but they didn't really believe (that is, they did not accept as true the facts that were reported or trust the report sufficiently to act accordingly). So they were lost. Peter and the apostles *believed in God,* accepted as true what God had done in Christ, and therefore trusted God more than men.

The early Christians accepted another aspect of faith, one that modern believers sometimes forget. They believed the facts about Christ, they entrusted their lives to Him, they were faithfully obedient to the demands of the gospel, and they lived as *members of the faith.* Those who had a common faith in Jesus as the Christ and who trusted their lives to Him were thrown together in a company of believers. They were *of the faith.* Acts speaks of "the company of those who believed" (4:32). The believers not only had a faith in Christ in common; they had one another in common, having been drawn together into a community of faith. Their allegiance to Christ brought them together.

Repentance
When God calls through His prophets for His people to repent, He is urging them to turn away from their pursuit of false gods, whether those gods be Baal or Moloch or power or sex or money or self-indulgence. He wants the pretentious to bow

26

down, the phony to become honest, the lustful to learn love; He desires the subjects of the kingdom of the world to renounce this dark domain and become citizens of the kingdom of God, to live in His light and in the love of His people. He wants to break the tyranny of sin, error, sickness, and death over human personalities; His plan is to banish fear forever. He hopes the lonely, orphaned soul will find a permanent home in the household of God.

John the Baptist did not introduce a new theme when he appeared in the wilderness of Judea crying, "Repent . . ." He stood in a long line of prophets who likewise called out, "Repent and turn away from your idols; and turn away your faces from all your abominations. . . . Repent and turn from all your transgressions, lest iniquity be your ruin" (Ezekiel 14:6; 18:30). John's warning was not new, but when he urged repentance because the kingdom of Heaven was at hand, he was preparing the way for a new day. God was about to make it possible for sinful men to escape the clutches of this world and dwell in a new and unprecedented kingdom, one not *of* yet *in* this world. A new day was coming, with a new Lord to rule in the new kingdom.

When the new Lord appeared, He began His ministry with the same message John was preaching: "Repent, for the kingdom of heaven is at hand." Even as He taught so thoroughly about this kingdom throughout His days on earth, He never ceased calling for a genuine turning toward God. Centuries later the brilliant mathematician and Christian thinker Pascal summarized two central teachings of the Christian religion, the need for repentance and the need for God through Christ to make it possible for us to become part of His kingdom:

> The Christian religion teaches men these two truths; that there is a God whom men can know, and that there is a corruption in their nature which renders them unworthy of Him. It is equally important to men to know both these points; and it is dangerous for men to know God without knowing his own wretchedness, and to know his own wretchedness, without knowing the Redeemer who can free him from it.

We need to be made aware of our corrupted selves so that we humbly allow Christ to rescue us from corruption and place us securely in the kingdom of God.

Repentance therefore incorporates several meanings. At its simplest it means to change one's mind, to turn from one belief or opinion to another. Like belief, though, repentance is not just an intellectual exercise. It involves one's emotional nature, causing "godly sorrow" or regret. It also is a moral change, a turning from delight in sin and its enticements to delight in God and His pleasure. It is a turnabout in attitude from rebellion to obedience. It naturally affects one's social life, for the penitent believer will avoid keeping company that will entice him to disobey God; he will turn eagerly toward new companions who are also trying to please God.

In the Old Testament Israel falls under the judgment of God when straying from obedience to Him; the nation can return to God's favor only through repentance. Days of national repentance are described in Nehemiah 9; individuals may also repent and turn to God (see 1 Kings 21), sometimes carrying out rituals of repentance (fasting, tearing one's clothes, putting on sackcloth and ashes). If the repentance is genuine, it is demonstrated in a godly, obedient life, one not dependent upon ritual or sacrifice but evident in a renewed heart and spirit (Amos 5:21-24; Ezekiel 18:31).

John's preaching at the Jordan continued the prophetic tradition. What was new in John's ministry was not his preaching, but his relating the message of repentance and the kingdom of God to baptism for the forgiveness of sins. He demanded not only sorrow for their sins, but a turning toward God and bringing their lives under His sovereign will; their baptism evidenced their repentant spirits and their yielding to God's will.

Even the casual New Testament student is impressed with the resemblance between John's preaching and the early message of Jesus. At the first the words are the same, but then Jesus' demands become more radical: "Unless you turn and become like children, you will never enter the kingdom of heaven" (Matthew 18:3); "Unless one is born anew, he cannot see the kingdom of God" (John 3:3); "Whoever of you does not renounce all that he has cannot be my disciple" (Luke 14:33). His major assignment, He says to the disgust of the Pharisees, is not "to call the righteous, but sinners to repentance" (Luke 5:32). As far as Jesus is concerned, faith and repentance are two sides of the same coin. Once one believes that Jesus is the Son of God, he will want to bring himself under the lordship of the

King of Heaven. He cannot limp along with partial allegiance to this world and partial loyalty to his new King; either he will renounce this world's hold on him or he will not. Repentance is renunciation of citizenship in the kingdom of this world and a pledge of allegiance to the new kingdom.

Since repentance was the inescapable demand in Jesus' preaching, it is no wonder that the apostolic church carried the theme forward so vigorously. Peter was only following Christ's example when he exhorted his Pentecost audience to repent. (See also Acts 3:19; 5:31; 8:22; 2 Corinthians 7:9; Hebrews 6:1; and Revelation 2:21.) The fact that repentance encompasses one's whole personality is inherent in Paul's noble appeal for personality transformation. He does not use the word repent, but his exhortation offers the finest definition we could use to conclude this discussion of repentance:

> I appeal to you therefore, brethren, by the mercies of God, to present your bodies as a living sacrifice, holy and acceptable to God, which is your spiritual worship. Do not be conformed to this world but be transformed by the renewal of your mind, that you may prove what is the will of God, what is good and acceptable and perfect (Romans 12:1, 2).

For Further Consideration

1. What is the difference between *being sorry* and *repenting?* (See 2 Corinthians 7:9-11; Matthew 3:8)
2. What does being *saved* mean?
3. What is the difference between the way one is saved and the way one becomes a member of the church in the book of Acts?
4. In the salvation process, what are the two gifts that only God can give?
5. What specifically did the term *believer* mean when applied to New Testament Christians? That is, what did they believe?
6. *Faith* means belief. What else does it mean?
7. What does a person's faith in God suggest about his relationships with others who have faith in God?
8. What was the role of John the Baptist and his message of repentance?
9. What are the several meanings of repentance?
10. What was the message of Jesus' early ministry?

CHAPTER THREE

Getting Into the Church: Baptism, Forgiveness, and the Holy Spirit

Any study of Christian baptism should begin with a reminder that baptism does not stand alone as the means to salvation. "For by grace you have been saved through faith; and this is not your own doing, it is the gift of God" (Ephesians 2:8). The relationship of baptism and grace is often distorted. We must remember that baptism is not

—a work by which one earns his salvation. The Bible does not teach baptismal regeneration (that is, that one can be saved by baptism alone).

—a meaningless sign that can be dispensed with. Some who see very clearly that one cannot earn salvation by a work called baptism then go to the opposite extreme of dismissing the rite as meaningless and unnecessary.

—a requirement for membership in some churches, which is otherwise irrelevant to one's being in Christ.

Although, as we shall see, baptism has many purposes, we can safely say that it is at least a twofold sign. First, it is a sign of what God is doing for us. As we are immersed in the enveloping waters so God immerses us (bathes, surrounds us) with His promised Holy Spirit. Secondly, it is a sign of what we are doing. Basically, in baptism we are doing nothing except yielding ourselves to the water and the one who is administering the rite. There is no *work* involved in baptism at all. The candidate is the passive recipient of the good offices of the one who baptizes, just as he is the recipient of the grace of God that saves him.

Our understanding of baptism becomes enlightened when we look at the many Scriptures on the subject. With their help we can see the complex meaning of this simple act. There are many purposes, but there is only one baptism (Ephesians 4:5).

—Baptism is for the forgiveness of sins (Acts 2:38).
—Baptism is an appeal for a clear conscience (1 Peter 3:20, 21).
—Baptism is the means of uniting with, or putting on, Christ (Galatians 3:27; Romans 6:3-5).
—Baptism is an agent in one's being born again (John 3:5; Romans 6:4; Titus 3:5).
—Baptism is associated with receiving the Holy Spirit (Matthew 3:13-17; John 3:5; Titus 3:5; 1 Corinthians 12:13).
—Baptism is the burial of one's past and resurrection into a new life (Romans 6:1-11). Baptism points not only to Christ's death, but to ours as well. As Christ rose from the grave to live forever, so shall we.
—Baptism is one's initiation into membership in the body of Christ (1 Corinthians 12:13; Acts 2:38-42). In the New Testament times, it was inconceivable for one to be in Christ and not in His body, the church.
—Baptism follows immediately upon one's acceptance of the gospel and penitent desire to accept Christ as Lord and Savior (Acts 2:38; 2:41; 8:12, 36-38; 9:18; 10:48; 16:15, 33; 18:8; 19:5; 22:16).

One of the most famous Scriptures in the Bible is Christ's final commission to His disciples, Matthew 28:18-20. Some modern Biblical scholars doubt the authenticity of the passage, in spite of the fact that it is found in all the major manuscripts, but there seems to be little reason to doubt that these are Jesus' words:

All authority in heaven and on earth has been given to me. Go therefore and make disciples of all nations, baptizing them in the name of the Father and of the Son and of the Holy Spirit, teaching them to observe all that I have commanded you; and lo, I am with you always, to the close of the age.

The use of the triune formula (Father, Son, and Holy Spirit) is what causes doubt, since other passages regarding baptism show that the early Christians were baptized in the name of Jesus only. That point can be debated; what is beyond debate, however, is that Jesus' disciples were commissioned to make other disciples everywhere and that the discipling process involved baptism and teaching. Their baptism was the obvious turning point in the new disciples' life. Before baptism they were perceived as belonging to the world; after baptism, to Christ.

We haven't said much about the mode of baptism so far. Immersion has been assumed, because immersion was the only form of baptism in the beginning. The verb *baptizo* in pre-Christian as well as Christian Greek means "to plunge, sink, drown, drench, overwhelm, dip, immerse." Never does it mean "to sprinkle or to pour." Paul used *baptizo* in its usual sense when he applied it as a figure of speech, saying that the Israelites were "baptized into Moses in the cloud and in the sea" (1 Corinthians 10:2). Their immersion into the cloud and sea was like being united with Moses, as our immersion in the water signifies our union with Christ.

Romans 6 speaks of baptism as our death, burial and resurrection. It is this drama that immersion enacts. One does not need to be a theologian or even a literate person to understand what is being demonstrated when a believer is immersed. He can see the burial and the rising again; he already knows the cleansing properties of water; he recognizes that this simple act signifies a real departure for the baptized person, a change of his life's direction. And when he learns that all the Christians surrounding him have also been immersed, he recognizes the act as a rite of initiation and acceptance into the larger body of believers. No substitute for immersion can communicate as much.

Immersion remained the mode of baptism, even in the Roman Catholic church, for more than 1200 years. At the Council of Ravenna in 1311 the Roman church officially legalized sprinkling but left the choice between that and immersion to the officiating minister. With every major reform movement that has taken the New Testament as the norm for the church, immersion has been recommended as the proper mode of baptism. Martin Luther said, "Baptism is a Greek word and may be translated immerse. I would have those who are to be baptized to be altogether dipped." John Wesley's *Notes on the New Testament* comment on Romans 6:4, "We are buried with him—alluding to the ancient manner of baptizing by immersion." Contemporary New Testament churches follow the same practice.

This form of burial makes sense for a person of accountable age, for he has lived long enough to know what sin is and to want release from its grip. He has personally disappointed God and himself and wants to be freed from his guilty conscience. Baptism is the cleansing act to which a believer submits; all the Scriptures studied above presuppose that immersion is the voluntary act of a free moral agent acting without coercion. He wants a new life in Christ; he gives himself over freely to the will of the Lord. Baptism is thus not for infants who can neither believe nor repent; it is for those old enough to recognize their accountability to God and want to be in harmony with His will. Although the New Testament mentions household baptisms (in which all the members of the household are baptized), infants are nowhere mentioned. A strong case for baptizing babies or young children cannot be built from the silence of the Scriptures; to do so strongly suggests that one believes in salvation by baptism, since in the case of an infant neither faith nor repentance is possible.

The meaning of baptism was demonstrated by a young couple who had been visiting our worship services for several weeks. I knew just a little of their background. Since both of them came from denominations that practice sprinkling as baptism, neither person had been immersed into Christ. I thought they were hesitating to become members of our church because of our practice of immersion. When the wife told me that she wanted to become a member but her husband was not ready, I asked him whether baptism was holding him back. His answer was exactly what I wanted to hear.

"No," he said, "the problem isn't baptism. You know, we have joined several churches over the years, but it has always been a matter of signing a card and we were in. We have been attending your church for several weeks now and we know that there is something different about it. You don't want people just to join your church. What you are after is total commitment to Christ, isn't it?"

"That's it!" I assured him, with more enthusiasm than dignity. "That's exactly what we want."

"I realize that once I make my commitment to Christ, baptism is no problem at all. I'll want to be baptized."

Baptism is not really an issue for those who are ready to commit their lives fully to the Lord Jesus Christ. They will want to do what He did, obey what He commands, become what He desires of them. The real issue is, "Will you or will you not give your heart to Christ?" If you will, then your baptism into Him will signify the total turnaround in your life.

We have been tracing the implications of Peter's instructions to his Pentecost audience to "Repent and be baptized." We have examined the meaning of repentance and baptism and of the faith upon which both of them are based. But Peter not only commanded his hearers to respond; he also promised them forgiveness of their sins and the gift of the Holy Spirit. Let's look very briefly at these promises.

Forgiveness of Sins

Their immediate need, of course, was to escape the awful burden of guilt they now carried because of the inhumane and unjust execution of Jesus. Having the strong Jewish sense of community, they knew they were as guilty as the ones who had actually done the dirty work. They needed some way to cleanse themselves. So Peter's instructions were welcome relief to them.

They were not alone in their guilt, however. Peter's generous offer of forgiveness came from God himself to all mankind. "For God so loved the world that he gave his only Son, that whoever believes in him should not perish but have eternal life." God's purpose in Christ was to save, not to condemn, but "since all have sinned and fall short of the glory of God" (Romans 3:23), nothing short of Christ's sacrifice could effectively erase human guilt. Through Christ God offers the required forgiveness.

So deep is the human longing for forgiveness that it is no wonder the cross has become the most popular symbol of the Christian faith. It represents what God has done for us in Christ. As the two bars of the cross meet, so it represents the meeting point of man's need and God's love, man's guilt and God's forgiveness. The cross is our constant reminder that "God was in Christ reconciling the world to himself, not counting their trespasses against them" (2 Corinthians 5:19). Jesus subjected himself to death on a cross in order to save us.

He hoped to save all of us. Here is the greatest mystery of all. Forgiveness is offered by Peter not only to those in his immediate audience "but to all who are far off;" it is offered not only to the good people or the nearly righteous, but to the outcast, the reject, the grossest of sinners. Through Christ's forgiveness murderers have been reclaimed, alcoholics rehabilitated, thieves reformed. When they have realized that God's grace is extended even to them, they have received His forgiveness and become His new creatures. A young woman, for example, was rushed to a hospital emergency room after having been stabbed in a drunken brawl. The doctors' diagnosis was the worst. They could not save her. A nurse was assigned to sit with her until the end came.

As the nurse studied the girl's hard face her patient opened her eyes. "I want you to tell me something and tell me straight," she said. "Do you think God cares about people like me? Do you think He could forgive anyone as bad as me?" Because of the cross the nurse could tell her, after she prayed for the right words, that God indeed did care for her and could forgive her. That is the *good news* about Christ—He wants to forgive and rescue even "people like me—as bad as me."

The conscientious believers who heard Peter on that Pentecost were as stricken as the young girl—and perhaps as doubtful that God could forgive them for rejecting and killing His Son. They appealed to Peter to tell it to them straight. Could God forgive people as bad as they? That is precisely what Peter offered them. Later Paul would summarize this startling offer in these words:

> While we were yet helpless, at the right time Christ died for the ungodly. Why, one will hardly die for a righteous man—though perhaps for a good man one will dare even to die. But God shows his love for us in that while we were yet sinners Christ died for us (Romans 5:6-8).

This was new to the Jews. The God of Judaism had always been willing to forgive, of course, but His forgiveness was primarily for the person who had changed his ways, made restitution for what he had done wrong, offered a sacrifice, and evidenced his repentance in a reformed life. First the change, then the offer of forgiveness. But with Jesus the order was reversed: first the offer of forgiveness and acceptance into the family of God, then the changed life.

Further, with Christians forgiveness is not something to be repeated indefinitely for constantly repeated sins. What is offered is forgiveness plus victory over sins. The power of sin has been conquered through the blood of the Lamb. There is nothing cheap about this forgiveness; if there were, we would be tempted to continue in our sins "that grace may abound" (see Romans 6:1). What Peter offers is forgiveness of sin and the power over the sins forgiven. To take the forgiveness without the power would lead to moral weakness; to accept the forgiveness and the power leads to life victorious.

It is practically impossible to say too much about this gift. Unfortunately, a study book like this one spends a disproportionate time explaining the more difficult concepts like repentance and faith when we would rather celebrate the marvels of the guilt-free life Peter promises. To know that God will erase our past records and set us free from all our yesterdays is incentive enough to follow Peter's instructions gladly.

Gift of the Holy Spirit

Even more incredible than Peter's offer of forgiveness is his promise of the gift of the Holy Spirit. This is the power that promises victory over sin. Christ had foretold the coming of the Spirit to His original disciples, of course, because they were to carry out His rescue mission. But now Peter demonstrates the incredible generosity of God who is willing to give himself not only to the chosen few, but even "to you and to your children and to all that are far off, every one whom the Lord our God calls to him" (Acts 2:39). Through forgiveness the new Christian enters the church pure, as one declared innocent by God himself. Through the gift of the Holy Spirit he now has the power to remain innocent, to accomplish the will of God in his life, to tell others of the new life he has found in Christ, and to grow into Christlikeness. Sin no more has power over him; he is strong enough through the Holy Spirit to triumph over the temptations and influences that used to control his life.

This is good news indeed. In spite of ourselves, our best intentions are not good enough. We want to improve but we don't improve; we struggle to avoid temptation but we sin. We are overwhelmed by our own drives for self-preservation, sex, and power. Apparently our will is too weak to tame these forces. But they can be tamed by God; the Holy Spirit is God breaking in upon us—at our invitation—to bring our inner thoughts and desires and drives into unity with Him.

We tend to think of the Father as aloof and remote, the creator and judge of the universe. He is high and we are low; He is holy and we are not. He comes a little closer in the person of Jesus, who resembled us in so many ways yet was not entirely like us. Even His presence intimidates, however. But the Holy Spirit shows us another aspect of God. The Spirit is not high and lifted up, but here and close to us; He is not limited by flesh to one time and place, but can be as present to us in twentieth-century America as He was to first-century Christians. He is with us, in us, working through us.

William Temple once gave a helpful illustration of the Holy Spirit. He said that it was no use handing him Shakespeare's *Hamlet* or *King Lear* with instructions to write another play like one of them. He couldn't. Likewise, it would be a waste of time to show him a life like Jesus' with instructions to live like Him. He couldn't do that, either. But if the genius ("spirit") of Shakespeare could live in Temple, then he could write such plays. And if the Spirit of Jesus could live in him, then he could live a life like that of Jesus. What Peter promises is quite similar: it is nothing less than the Spirit of Jesus indwelling the newborn believer. Jesus is the supreme example; the Spirit of Jesus living in His disciple empowers him to follow the example.

The Holy Spirit, then, is God intimately and powerfully working in and through a disciple of Christ. He is the *paraklete*, a Greek word that is often translated *comforter*, but is also translated *mediator, intercessor, helper,* and *advocate*. He is the one who comes to the aid of the believer and stands with him in his defense. Bernard Ramm has helpfully translated the word by borrowing *ombudsman* from the Swedish. He notes that in the centuries before the birth of Christ the Roman government eased the tension between the rulers and the ruled by establishing a special office. A group of men were elected by the people to present their grievances to the government. These men, called the tribunes of the people, handled all kinds of complaints on their behalf.

Modern Scandinavians have instituted a similar office. The *ombudsman* presents the complaints of his people to the government. Ramm used this term to emphasize the fact that in his Christian pilgrimage the modern believer faces many problems that he cannot handle on his own. But God has not abandoned him. He has appointed the divine ombudsman to act on the believer's behalf in all troubled situations. Whatever need he has, the believer has the right to summon his ombudsman to his assistance.

The Holy Spirit has another duty, also. He also speaks on behalf of the believer to God. "We do not know how to pray as we ought," writes the apostle Paul, "but the Spirit himself intercedes for us with sighs too deep for words" (Romans 8:26). Thus the Christian has the Spirit's assistance before man and before God.

Furthermore, through the Spirit's gifts the believer can make his contribution to the ministry of the church, offering whatever the Spirit has given him as his gift in turn to the church (see 1 Corinthians 12:4-31). As a new Christian, the believer will want to assist the prosperity and unity of the entire body. So that all can do their share, "to each is given the manifestation of the Spirit for the common good," all these being "inspired by one and the same Spirit, who apportions to each one individually as he wills" (1 Corinthians 12:7, 11).

One who has been born of "water and the Spirit" (John 3:5) has thus entered into the kingdom of God, in which he walks by the Spirit (Romans 8:4), is helped in prayer by the same Spirit (Romans 8:26) and knows himself to be indwelt by that Spirit (1 Corinthians 3:16), who guarantees his inheritance in an eternal future not made with hands (2 Corinthians 5:5). The test of the presence of the Holy Spirit is not the ability to do some spectacular feat, but the presence of the Spirit's fruit, which is "love, joy, peace, patience, kindness, goodness, faithfulness, gentleness, self-control" (Galatians 5:22, 23).

Another promise, perhaps the best of all, is bound up in Peter's offer as explained by Paul:

> But if Christ is in you, although your bodies are dead because of

sin, your spirits are alive because of righteousness. If the Spirit of him who raised Jesus from the dead dwells in you, he who raised Christ Jesus from the dead will give life to your mortal bodies also through his Spirit which dwells in you (Romans 8:10, 11).

All this is possible because, when we received the Spirit we received the spirit of sonship. So

when we cry, "Abba! Father!" it is the Spirit himself bearing witness with our spirit that we are children of God, and if children, then heirs, heirs of God and fellow heirs with Christ, provided we suffer with him in order that we may also be glorified with him (Romans 8:15-17).

All this and more is implied in Peter's generous promise from God, "and you shall receive the gift of the Holy Spirit."

For Further Consideration

1. Baptism here is called a twofold sign. What does it signify?
2. Why can't baptism be considered a *work* that leads to salvation?
3. What are some of the many Biblical statements made about baptism?
4. Why does this chapter assume that immersion is the appropriate mode of baptism?
5. Why does baptism seem especially appropriate for adults and not for infants?
6. How does baptism dramatize one's commitment to Christ?
7. What has it meant to you to know that your sins have been forgiven?
8. Do you think we Christians have really grasped the importance of Christ's gift of the Holy Spirit in our lives?

CHAPTER FOUR

The Church Described

(1 Peter 2:1-10)

The study of the church might be easier if the Bible would provide a single definition for it. Then we could just read that definition ("The church of Christ is . . ."), agree to it, and proceed to the next subject.

But the Scriptures nowhere give such a precise denotation. Instead they do something better, leaving us with a richer, more complex comprehension of this divine/human organism. In place of a single definition we find several word pictures. No one of them is complete in itself, but together they illustrate God's purposes for the church much as a gallery of an artist's paintings conveys a more complete impression of his full intentions better than any single painting could.

In this chapter we shall examine the most important word pictures. As we begin we will quickly grasp this basic fact: *the church is persons.* It is misleading to think of buildings or organizations or programs or schools as the church. To say "I belong to First Church" does not refer to the building at the corner of Tenth and Maple, but indicates "I am a member of the congregation of believers who meet regularly in the building at Tenth and Maple." A fire or flood could destroy the meeting house but the church would remain untouched.

Our word study will also soon convince us of another fact: the congregation meeting at Tenth and Maple is not to be thought of as a piece or arm of the church. It *is* the church. Everything the church is and has can be found at First Church. Nothing is needed for the salvation of mankind that First Church cannot offer. In the meetings of that congregation the gospel is preached, sinners repent, faith is demonstrated, baptism is administered, the Lord's Supper is observed, the Scriptures are searched, the various ministries assigned to the church are performed, the Holy Spirit is at work, and Christ's commission to disciple the world is obeyed. When the apostle Paul writes to the church at Corinth or at Rome or at Philippi, he does not address each one as a section of the church. He speaks of them as "the church at . . .". Every congregation, which is related to all other Christian congregations in the bond of Christ, is fully the church and not dependent upon some other body to perform any essential churchly function on its behalf. In fact, the only way one can accurately understand the church is in terms of the local congregation.

This fact means, then, that there are no insignificant churches. Wherever a congregation of Christians assemble, whatever the size of the church (even if only two or three are gathered in Christ's name, Matthew 18:20), there is Christ in the midst of them. This further means that there are no insignificant Christians. Since the church is persons, called by God to be His special people, every person in the church is important.

With these facts in mind we are ready to tour the gallery of word pictures.

The first cluster of words exhibits the church as *persons who believe in Christ.* They teach that God has acted in Christ to save all whom He has called to himself. Those who have answered God's call have been bound together in an inseparable community of believers in Jesus as the Christ, God's Son. Through Christ we also have become children of God (John 1:12); we are the "company of those who believe" (Acts 4:32).

Biblical word pictures show the intensity and intimacy of our relationship with Christ. The church is called the *bride of Christ.* The New Testament freely borrows the language of love to describe the marriage of Christ and His church.

Christ loves the church as a husband loves his wife (Ephesians 5:25-27, 29).

We are betrothed to Christ, as a pure bride to her husband (2 Corinthians 11:2).

41

Jesus refers to himself as a groom (Matthew 9:15; 22:1-10). John the Baptist uses the same word for Christ (John 3:29).

Earth offers no more elevated relationship than that between husband and wife. A good marriage requires the very best of both man and woman, with each partner submitting and sacrificing for the sake of the other. That describes the bond of love uniting Christ and the church. This analogy to marriage is not new. The Old Testament prophets often presented the nation of Israel as God's betrothed (Hosea 2:20), wife (Isaiah 54:5, 6), and bride (Jeremiah 2:2). The prophets urged Israel not only to uphold the terms of her covenant with God, but to treat Him with the love, respect, and obedience due the divine Husband from His chosen beloved. The New Testament writers employ the same connotations in their use of the marriage analogy.

The church is also called the *body of Christ*, further emphasizing the unbreakable union of Christ and church. No one needs to point out the mutual dependence of all the members of our physical bodies upon one another and their reliance upon the head. Head and body are inseparable, with the body depending upon the head for the proper functioning of the whole organism. (See Ephesians 4:1-16; 5:23; Romans 12:4, 5; 1 Corinthians 12:4-27.)

A variation of this theme is found in another picture, that of the *vine and the branches*. In John 15:1-8 Jesus calls himself the *vine*, His followers the *branches*, and the Father the *vinedresser*. Branches cannot survive or bear fruit apart from the life-giving vine. There is no independent existence for rebellious or freethinking branches; apart from the vine they are dead. Certainly they cannot fulfill their purpose once they are severed from the vine. Many churches may have the appearance of a church, with splendid organization and active programs and imposing building, but without an intimate relationship with and dependence upon the Head of the church, the Vine of the branches, they are but dead imitations.

To a rural population Jesus' picture of the *shepherd with his flock* is an equally vivid illustration of the church's dependence upon Christ. Jesus assumes the role of shepherd (John 10:1-16) and instructs His disciple Peter to take care of His sheep (John 21:15-17). He sorrows over the leaderless and confused people, because they are "like sheep without a shepherd" (Matthew 9:36). The early church quickly picked up Christ's language, instructing the elders of the churches to care for their members like shepherds who care for sheep (see 1 Peter 5:2-4; Acts 20:28).

This cluster of words, then, portrays the church as persons intimately united with Christ. They believe in Him, they live and move and have their being in Him. Their devotion is not a casual affair. He is not only their teacher and prophet, as some prefer to call Him, but He is more: He is lover, friend, and supplier of every need, as necessary to their lives as food itself ("I am the bread of life"), protector from every danger. Christians are intimately, inseparably His.

Because the church is persons who are in Christ, it necessarily follows that church members are *persons who belong to God through Christ.* Jesus prayed that as He was in the Father, so those who would believe in Him would also be in God (John 17:21), since "all mine are thine" (John 17:10). Peter calls the church "God's own people" (1 Peter 2:9, 10). Other versions indicate the richness of this phrase: "a peculiar people" (King James Version); "a people of His acquisition" (Modern Language Bible); "you are God's very own" (Living Bible).

First Peter 2:9 spells out what it means to be the people of God:

You are a chosen race. You have been selected by God for His special purposes. The church is not an organization invented by men for human purposes, but the handiwork of God's creativity. Paul picks up this theme in 2 Corinthians 6:16-18, freely quoting from the Old Testament and applying God's words to the church: For we are the temple of the living God; as God said,

> I will live in them and move among them,
> > and I will be their God,
> > and they shall be my people.
> Therefore come out from them,
> > and be separate from them, says the Lord,
> > and touch nothing unclean;
> then I will welcome you,
> > and I will be a father to you,
> > and you shall be my sons and daughters,
> > says the Lord Almighty.

The church is His people, tied to Him by a New Covenant, as surely as the people of Israel were His through His covenant with Moses (see Hebrews 8:8-13). In both cases, God did the selecting. We are His people through His choosing, not our own.

God's sovereignty in selecting His chosen people is sometimes usurped, however. If this historical tidbit can be trusted, a New England assembly met in 1640 to consider three resolutions. The presumptuous minutes read:

1. The earth is the Lord's and the fullness thereof. Voted.
2. The Lord may give the earth or any part of it to His chosen people. Voted.
3. We are His chosen people. Voted.

One wonders how God voted on the third motion.

You are a royal priesthood. In the church every member is a priest, offering himself as a sacrifice to God (Romans 12:1; 1 Peter 2:5) as the Old Testament priests offered cereal and burnt offerings on behalf of their people. Because of what Christ our high priest has done, we can enter the sanctuary and draw near to God without any human intermediary (Hebrews 10:19-21). Instead of requiring the services of a priest to intercede for us, we have become priests ourselves.

During much of Hebrew history, the tabernacle or temple was the focal point of worship, with the priests there officiating on behalf of their people. But with the coming of Christ, the focus changed. God cannot be confined to any location or temple, Jesus taught (John 4), since God is spirit. The Spirit does not reside in buildings of stone, but in persons ("living stones," 1 Peter 2:5). The church has become a new *temple of the Holy Spirit,* for the church is persons who believe in Christ and have yielded themselves to Him through faith and repentance, being baptized in His name and receiving the Holy Spirit. (See Acts 2:38; 1 Corinthians 3:16, 17; 6:19; 2 Corinthians 6:16; Ephesians 2:21, 22.)

You are a holy nation. As the nation of Israel was holy ("set apart") to God, different from any other people on earth, designed to be a blessing to all humanity, so the church is now a sacred nation above nations, not bound by any racial or nationalistic distinctions but sprinkled like salt to bless all mankind. This nation is a *kingdom* whose sovereign is God (1 Thessalonians 2:12), who presides over a realm that cannot be shaken (Hebrews 12:28; Matthew 16:18). It is the *new Israel* (Galatians 6:16; Hebrews 8:8-13), comprised of persons whose hearts belong to God, spiritual sons of Abraham.

> For we are the true circumcision, who worship God in spirit, and glory in Christ Jesus, and put no confidence in the flesh (Philippians 3:3).

> So you see that it is men of faith who are the sons of Abraham (Galatians 3:7).

> See also Colossians 2:11, 12; Galatians 3:23; 4:7; Romans 4:1-16.

If a nation is holy, it then follows that its citizens will also be called holy. So Christians wear the name *saint* in the New Testament, a word meaning *holy one*, separated or set apart to God. Church members are called to be special, separated from sin and from other people (having a different God and different values). In 2 Thessalonians 1:10 "his saints" refers to "all who have believed." Their very belief in God through Christ has separated them from nonbelievers. Therefore when Paul writes to his fellow Christians in other cities, he addresses them as "the saints who are at . . ." (See Romans 1:7; 1 Corinthians 1:2; 2 Corinthians 1:1; Ephesians 1:1, etc.) He is writing to a select group of citizens within the cities, men and women whom God has set apart from the populace at large, in order that they may carry out His redemptive plans.

The church, then, is persons who belong to God through Christ. But more than this, *Christians also belong to one another*.

The term *church (ekklesia)* means "called out . . . to be an assembly, community, or congregation." God has not called us to live solitary Christian lives, isolated from one another, but to live in close fellowship. The *ekklesia* is an assembly of persons chosen by God, always clustered around the One who called them together. The church therefore can never be defined as an unchanging institution, but as a gathering of those who are answering God's constant call to come to himself. Their answer to His call brings and holds them together. If they desire to be in the presence of God they must remain in the presence of each other.

The uses of *church* are so frequent that they do not require further comment, but the sense of our belonging to one another is perhaps best grasped by another word picture, that of the church as a *household* or *family*. First Peter 2:5 calls the church a *spiritual house*. This term by itself seems a bit ambiguous, but when placed in the company of the following, its meaning becomes clear.

> . . . you may know how one ought to behave in the *household of God,* which is the church of the living God (1 Timothy 3:15).

> So then you are no longer strangers and sojourners, but you are fellow citizens with the saints and members of the *household of God* (Ephesians 2:19).

> But when the time had fully come, God sent forth his Son, born of woman, born under the law, to redeem those who were under the law, so that we might receive *adoption as sons* (Galatians 4:4, 5).

> But to all who received him, who believed in his name, he gave power to become *children of God* . . . (John 1:12).

> For you did not receive the spirit of slavery to fall back into fear, but you have received the *spirit of sonship*. When we cry, "Abba! Father!" it is the Spirit himself bearing witness with our spirit that we are *children of God,* and if children, then heirs, *heirs of God* and *fellow heirs with Christ,* provided we suffer with him in order that we may also be glorified with him (Romans 8:15-17).

We are right, then, to call our local congregation a family, *the* family of God. We are born into the family by water and the spirit (John 3:5), we eat our family meals (breaking of bread), we wear and try to bring honor to the family name (Christian), we are obedient to the Head of the family and carry out His wishes. We did not somehow earn the right to belong to the family, but were selected and adopted by the Father who wanted us to be His children.

In this context it would be good to look again at a picture we mentioned earlier. The term the *body of Christ* not only points to the inseparable relationship between Christ and the church, as noted above, but it also characterizes the family relationship of the members. They belong to each other as much as nose goes with eyes. To be a member of the family of God, or the body of Christ, is to belong to every other member. No member can say to another, as Paul makes so clear in 1 Corinthians 12, 'I have nothing to do with you.' Charles Schulz, the creator of the Peanuts cartoon, illustrates this theme with Snoopy. Everybody's favorite dog is sitting on his doghouse nursing a bandaged foot. He explains that his body blames his foot for not being able to go places, his foot says it is all his head's fault, and his head blames his eyes and his eyes accuse his feet of clumsiness, and his right foot says not to blame him for what his left foot has done. But Snoopy remains aloof from it all. "I don't say anything because I don't want to be involved!" The humor, of course, is in the impossibility of Snoopy's conclusion. He is already involved; he belongs to his body. If we belong to Christ's body, God's family, we are involved with one another whether we like it or not.

This sense of our belonging to one another and to God is intensified by another frequently used word. We are *slaves* or *servants*, imitating Christ who "emptied himself, taking the form of a servant" (Philippians 2:7) when He came in the likeness of men. The task of the church is not to elevate the members, but to preach "Jesus Christ as Lord, *with ourselves as your servants* for Jesus' sake" (2 Corinthians 4:5). Even though Christians have been set free from bondage to sin and legalism, we do not use our freedom as license but through love seek to "be servants of one another" (Galatians 5:13). Martin Luther correctly illustrates this paradox of Christian freedom when he writes, "A Christian is a perfectly free lord of all, subject to none; a Christian is a perfectly dutiful servant of all, subject to all."

Slavery is not a new condition for us. Before our conversion, we were slaves of sin and unrighteousness; we were destined to die. But then, thank God, we were confronted with a choice of masters:

> Do you not know that if you yield yourselves to any one as obedient slaves, you are slaves of the one whom you obey, either of sin, which leads to death, or of obedience, which leads to righteousness? But thanks be to God, that you who were once slaves of sin have become obedient from the heart to the standard of teaching to which you were committed, and, having been set free from sin, have become *slaves of righteousness* (Romans 6:16-18).

This means, of course, that "you have been set free from sin and have become slaves of God" (Romans 6:22).

In our serving, we are merely imitating Jesus.

A disciple is not above his teacher, nor a servant above his master; it is enough for the disciple to be like his teacher, and the servant like his master (Matthew 10:24, 25).

Whoever would be first among you must be slave of all. For the Son of man also came not to be served but to serve, and to give his life as a ransom for many (Mark 10:44, 45).

We have not looked at all of the word pictures in the Biblical gallery. Other pictures tempt us to stay awhile longer, to study the church as salt and light, as soldiers and conquerors, as yeast that leavens and fishnets that catch. But enough has been said to describe the height and breadth and depth of this divine/human agency of God's love. One final word demands our consideration, however. Through all that we have seen, one theme remains constant from picture to picture. These persons who constitute the church are not what they once were. When they became Christ's, they were made new. And in Christ, they remain new.

Like *newborn babes,* long for the pure spiritual milk . . . (1 Peter 2:2).

From now on, therefore, we regard no one from a human point of view; even though we once regarded Christ from a human point of view, we regard him thus no longer. Therefore, if any one is in Christ, *he is a new creation;* the old has passed away, behold, the new has come (2 Corinthians 5:16, 17).

Remember that you were at that time separated from Christ, alienated from the commonwealth of Israel, and strangers to the covenants of promise, having no hope and without God in the world. But now in Christ Jesus you who once were far off have been brought near in the blood of Christ . . . that he might create in himself *one new man* in place of the two . . . (Ephesians 2:12-15).

Members of the church of Christ, then, cannot be equated with members of any other organization. They are no longer merely human; they have been reconstituted, recreated. As men and women in Christ, they have become ageless, having the innocence and vitality of children and the wisdom and stability of maturity. They live in a spiritual dimension and are no longer victims of the bonds of this world. They have been born again.

For Further Consideration

1. What makes your local church so important?
2. What does the name "bride of Christ" suggest to you about the character of the church? What about the "body of Christ"?
3. If you were to give a modern, urban equivalent of the shepherd with his flock, what would it be?
4. Does your church live up to God's expectation of it as a chosen race, a royal priesthood, a holy nation?
5. What does being a *saint* mean today? What should the term mean?
6. The church is called a family. Is this how we think of it, or do we tend to think of it more as an organization?
7. In what ways are we Christians involved with one another as members of the body?
8. Luther's paradox—perfect freedom, perfect servitude—is not easy to apply, is it? Do you have any suggestions?

CHAPTER FIVE

Church Members and Disciples

(Acts 2:41-47)

I recently picked up a book in an airport newsstand. Because of its bright fuchsia cover and daring title, I couldn't resist. *If You Meet the Buddha on the Road, Kill Him,* the title shouted. The rest of the cover hooked me: "No meaning that comes from outside ourselves is real. The Buddhahood of each of us has already been attained." The back cover was equally provocative: "The most important things that each man must learn, no one else can teach him." If these claims are true, then it would be a waste of time to read this book—or any other book. But I don't believe this and know the author doesn't either, or he would not have wasted his time writing a book from which no one else could learn.

It sounds appealing, doesn't it, this doctrine of self-sufficiency? If only everything we need to know really were locked up inside us, just waiting to be released. Too bad it isn't so. But you don't have to live very long before you discover, usually the hard way, that the most important knowledge in life does not come from within us; we learn it from others. That is why we need a teacher.

Unfortunately, it is now possible in some places to be recognized as a respectable church member without being a genuine disciple of Christ. Such persons are somewhat like the rather portly lady in a George Clark cartoon who explained to her friend, "My reducing club is a great success. We've lost 148 pounds. However, none of it is mine personally." Without personal involvement, some church members keep their names on the membership list and even boast about the fine accomplishments of their church—although they have not contributed to the success personally. They want to have a church, however, for assistance at births, marriages, and deaths (for "hatching, matching, and dispatching," a friend of mine says). What these church members have not understood is that membership without discipleship is an insult to Jesus and a repudiation of His teaching.

If such membership is meaningless, then what *should* church members do? To answer, we must return again to the first days as recorded in Acts 2:41-47. When the three thousand souls responded to Peter's appeal, the church of Christ came into being. Those three thousand knew immediately that they had been introduced to the true Master; Peter spoke the truth and the Holy Spirit confirmed it. They believed then that God had sent Jesus to save them, teach them, and guide them into abundant life. When the new converts "were added" to the Lord and to one another, they were acknowledging Jesus as their leader and master. There was nothing casual or nominal about their commitment. They called Him Lord and themselves disciples.

We need to examine this word *disciple*. It is not used in Acts 2, but we learn in Acts 11:26 that it is synonymous with the later term *Christian*. It is used 232 times in the Gospels and can be counted 27 times in the book of Acts. It does not occur in the epistles; there the predominant word for Christian is *saint* (which occurs 57 times in the epistles and Revelation). *Disciple* means student, learner, or apprentice; it was commonly used in Greek and Roman society to designate the followers of a philosopher like Aristotle or Seneca; *saint* is a little broader term, indicating one who has been set apart by God for His special purposes.

We'll concentrate on *disciple* in this chapter, since we comfortable twentieth-century Christians need to recapture the challenge of its meaning. We recall that Jesus did not commission His followers to "go into all the world and make church members" with our compromised modern understanding of church membership. He ordered them to make *disciples*, which is His definition of church membership. Henry Ward Beecher has described a Christian as "nothing but a sinful man who has put himself to school to Christ for the honest purpose of becoming better." There is more to the Christian life than what Beecher suggests, but he does capture the essence of discipleship with his "man who has put himself to school to Christ." As soon as the earliest converts had followed Peter's instructions in repentance and baptism, they formed themselves into "little schools" or groups of apprentices in order to study the apostles' teaching, break bread, pray, and share their lives. Their meetings were punctuated by marvels and praises and unselfish joy. These "schools" were called churches.

The new disciples naturally wanted to learn from the *apostles' teaching* everything they could about their new Lord. They had accepted the fact that Jesus was the promised one of God, but they did not yet know much about Him. The New Testament had not been written, of course, so they had to rely for instruction upon pre-Christian Scriptures and the testimony of the apostles and others who had known Christ firsthand. They wanted to fulfill Christ's expectation: "If you continue in my word, you are truly my disciples, and you will know the truth, and the truth will make you free" (John 8:31, 32). So they were eager to learn what the apostles could teach them as they went "to school to Christ."

When they met together they not only studied; they also devoted themselves to the *breaking of bread*. This familiar phrase refers to two important elements in their church life. The first is simply their meeting regularly in each other's homes to eat, with each family bringing something for the shared meal, much like our "potluck" or "pitch in" dinners. At the meal, in accordance with the ancient laws of hospitality, every participant was treated as an equal and experienced unity in Christ with the other members. Nothing expresses friendship better than eating together.

In addition to the common meal, the Christians participated in a Communion service (variously referred to as "the breaking of bread" or "the Lord's Supper," or the Eucharist). Communion will be discussed more fully in a subsequent chapter. Here it is sufficient to note that it was customary at the close of the common meal for the recognized leader of the group to break bread and distribute it prayerfully to the members, and to ask a blessing on a cup of wine that he offered to each member.

This simple act, reminiscent of Jesus' upper room meal with His disciples, reminded these new disciples of Jesus' sacrificial love for them. It was also a dramatized lesson in discipleship: to be disciples of Christ they had to be prepared to take up their own cross and follow Him (Matthew 10:38). They had become citizens of the kingdom of Heaven; even their earthly lives had become expendable for righteousness' sake.

Through their devotion to *prayer* the new disciples kept in personal touch with their Master. They had been faithful Jews or believers in the one God before becoming Christians, so discipline in prayer was not new to them. They had always prayed, but now they added to their prayers the name of Jesus; in His name they addressed God and through Him they worshiped. In the temple daily, in their homes, and privately they talked with God. A disciple stays close to his Lord.

The meaning of their *fellowship* requires a full discussion which we shall postpone until later chapters.

The new disciples continued steadfastly in these disciplines because they had apprenticed themselves to Jesus; they wanted to become like Him even to the point, if necessary, of carrying their cross as He carried His. They concentrated on Him as Thomas Carlyle, the nineteenth-century author, gave his attention to the subject on whose biography he was working. It was his practice, we are told, to place a photograph of the subject before him, so that the character, who was never out of his sight while he was writing, became a living breathing reality, inspiring Carlyle in his work. Just so the disciples kept the image of Christ before themselves, wanting to know Him more fully, hoping they could become like Him.

When Jesus called His first disciples, Peter and Andrew, James and John and the others left their tasks to follow Him, not knowing where He was leading them. All they knew was that He was the only person they had ever met who was absolutely worthy of being their leader. One fact they quickly discovered: the life of a disciple is not a sedentary one. Jesus did not call them to occupy a pew. He made them pilgrims. To be one of Christ's is to walk where He leads. The Christian life is an adventure in faith; the excitement is that we are on our way but we're not sure where we are going. Our ultimate destiny is certain, but the journey there is uncertain. Our only assurance is that our Master knows. His is to lead, ours is to follow.

When the famed historian Samuel E. Morrison began writing his life of Columbus, *Admiral of the Ocean Sea*, he decided that the best preparation for writing would be to travel over the course of Columbus' actual voyages, in a sailing ship about the size of the Santa Maria. His goal, he said, was "to relive the discoveries of the great discoverer." What an adventure that must have been for Morrison. That is the adventure of a disciple who sets out to follow the footsteps of Jesus: he discovers the revelations of the Great Revealer.

His way is not always easy. It is not for the frivolous. Persons who are content with just holding a job and making a decent living, or puttering with some pleasurable hobbies and pastimes, do not find the disciplined Christian life attractive. Disciples are serious enough about life to want to learn all they can from its Master. They are not guilty of Kierkegaard's acute judgment:

> Ah, when some day the reckoning shall be made of the countless multitude of the human race, there will be found a greater number under the rubric "The flabby," than under all these rubrics taken together: "Thieves," "Robbers," "Murderers."

The flabby shall not inherit the kingdom of Heaven.

Christians, then, are disciplined students of life who have been formed into a company of disciples to share all they have with one another as they follow Christ, their Master. They remain faithful to the pilgrim band, because they have learned that they cannot experience the fullness of life alone. Jesus had instructed them in the lifestyle they are to exhibit: "By this all men will know that you are my disciples, if you have love for one another" (John 13:35).

For the earliest Christians to be devoted to *fellowship*, as Acts 2:42 says they were, they had to practice unselfish love, *agape*, with one another. The extent to which they willingly went is described in Acts 2:44-46. They had everything in common; they sold their possessions and goods and distributed them to all, as any had need. Their hearts were generous; they took care of one another. It is no wonder that daily their numbers grew.

The implications for today's church could not be clearer. In a recent book, Sherwood Wirt, former editor of *Decision*, speaks of the futility of using such categories as strong or weak, big or small, warm or cold to describe churches. In his opinion, there are only loving churches or unloving ones. While the phenomenal growth of the Southern Baptists is usually attributed to the zeal of their members, and that of the Pentecostals to their exercise of special gifts of the Spirit, Wirt is convinced that they have grown only because their members really love one another. That is undoubtedly the best possible explanation.

In one respect our twentieth-century society is quite like first-century Jerusalem. There were then and are now very few places for persons to go where they would not be used, mistreated, and manipulated. In the church where there is real love, however, they are protected and nurtured. Once a person has pledged his allegiance to Christ he assumes responsibility for sharing what he is and has with his fellow disciples. Love demands no less. That is why John, writing as an extremely old man, distilled the years of his experience as a disciple into one earnest appeal, "Little children, let us not love in word or speech but in deed and truth." "Beloved, if God so loved us, we also ought to love one another" (1 John 3:18, 4:11). Of the early Christians it was said, "Behold how they love one another." They were fellow pilgrims marching heavenward, but marching hand in hand, never letting go of one another, lest one of the members fall by the wayside and die.

The new company of disciples quickly grew. Note Acts 2:47: "And the Lord added to their number day by day those who were being saved." Jump ahead to the sixth chapter, verse 7: "The word of God increased; and the number of the disciples multiplied greatly in Jerusalem." Throughout the book the growth continues. The church grew not just because the members held on to one another, but because they also reached out to pick up others along their pilgrimage. They wanted to let others outside their group in on the blessings they were receiving. This was no exclusive society for the few. Taking their cue from Jesus, whose parable of the good Samaritan had a lasting impact on the new disciples, and whose warnings of the judgment included His powerful picture of the division of the sheep and goats on the basis of their care for the helpless (Matthew 25:31-46; see Chapter Ten in this book), these disciples were quickly found in the temple, on the streets, in the homes of their neighbors and friends, sharing the good news that had transformed their lives. Afraid of no one, they burned with desire to save others as they had been saved.

Their motive was like that which Keith Miller describes in his book, *The Taste of New Wine*. Having grown up in a church that practiced what he called "legalistic scalp hunting," Miller decided as an adult that he would not talk about Christ to others but simply live a good Christian life. That would be the best witness he could give. Then one day he realized how selfish his decision had been. He was like a man in a hospital's dreadful disease ward who has been secretly healed by a great physician but who tells no one about his healing. Instead, he remains in the ward, appearing to the sick patients to be getting stronger and stronger. He even helps them, trying to make them more comfortable as they die, but still not sharing with them how he has been healed. The only really loving thing to do, Miller finally realized, would be to introduce them to the physician who had healed him so that they too could be made well.

That is the task of Jesus' disciples—to introduce the dying to the Great Physician so that He might heal them and invite them to join the pilgrim band of disciples who are following Him to life.

To do so disciples must go where the sick are. An impressive effort to do just that was attempted by a church that raised thousands of dollars to establish the "Lamb's Center for Girls" in New York's infamous Times Square. The program is designed to offer redemptive care and rehabilitation for the area's prostitutes and runaways. Many of these women are small-town girls who fled to the city—to their destruction. Others are city girls whom life has abused. The world sees them as criminals to be locked up, many men see them as bodies to be used up, but here is a church that sees them as precious persons for whom Christ died—to be lifted up. This is the work of disciples.

Disciples are not concerned about their respectability. Jesus was never criticized for mingling with society's reputable citizens; He was condemned because His friends were sinners and prostitutes and tax collectors. He wanted to lift them up. His disciples follow His example.

What do Christians do? What does it mean to be a disciple of Jesus? It means to do what the earliest Christians did, to attach ourselves to the Master of life in order to learn from Him how to live, to pledge ourselves to one another as a band of disciples, walking hand in hand on a heavenward pilgrimage. Disciples have so much love for Christ and for one another that it over-flows in concern for those not yet making the pilgrimage with us, persons we hope to lift up and welcome into our pilgrim band.

That's what Christians do.

For Further Consideration

1. What is wrong with a person's putting "Number One" first in his life?
2. What is a good modern synonym for *disciple?*
3. What are four disciplines named in Acts 2:42 to which the first Christians devoted themselves? Are these still good guidelines to follow in our discipleship?
4. In what ways is the Christian life a pilgrimage?
5. What do we mean, "the flabby shall not inherit the kingdom of Heaven"?
6. This definition of a Christian is given in the chapter: "Christians, then, are disciplined students of life who have been formed into a company of disciples to share all they have with one another as they follow Christ, their Master." Do you agree with this definition? Can you improve upon it?
7. Do you accept Sherwood Wirt's emphasis upon the importance of love in today's church?
8. What is the full task of Jesus' disciples?
9. What disciplines do you apply in order to qualify as a *disciple* of Jesus?

CHAPTER SIX

The Church and the Bible

(2 Timothy 3:10-17)

Everything we have studied in this book is based upon the assumption that today's church should be rooted in New Testament Scripture. The need for churches to be grounded in the Scriptures has become more apparent in recent years with the proliferation of unorthodox cults, all of which boast that theirs is the only way of truth and salvation. One of these cults shocked the entire world in 1978, when Jimmie Jones and 900 of his fanatical People's Temple followers in Jonestown, Guyana, fulfilled their suicide pact with bullets and poison. Believing Jones to be endowed with divine authority, they obeyed him in grisly death as they had obeyed him blindly in life.

Earlier in his ministry Jones claimed to be a gospel preacher, but as his hold over his disciples grew, he rejected the authority of the Bible and usurped all power to himself. First he presented himself as a preacher, then as a reincarnation of Jesus; in the end he assumed the name of God, claiming that it was he who created the heavens and the earth. According to a former associate, even before Jones had moved his operation from Indiana to California (and from there to Guyana) there were indications of his megalomania. "Too many people are looking at this instead of looking at me," he once shouted, throwing his Bible to the floor. By diverting his people's allegiance from the Bible to himself, Jones was at liberty to do with them whatever he pleased. His congregation was no longer a church of Christ, but Jimmie Jones' church.

When he scrapped the Bible and usurped its authority, Jones became one more of a large band of cultist leaders who have held the allegiance of their devotees by claiming to be God or to receive revelations directly from God. They offer new scriptures for old. Joseph Smith would have been nobody without his Book of Mormon, for which he claimed divine origin. When that proved insufficient, he began his series of "revelations" to bolster his hold on his followers. Mary Baker Eddy had to supply *Science and Religion with a Key to the Scriptures* in order to guarantee that her followers would support her teachings rather than the Scriptures alone. The Reverend Moon, the many Eastern gurus, and numerous other religious "prophets" continue to confuse the contemporary religious scene through their egocentric claims to be the Truly Enlightened One, *the* source of divine truth. Immature persons, unsure of their convictions and ungrounded in Biblical knowledge, are "tossed to and fro and carried about with every wind of doctrine, by the cunning of [these] men, by their craftiness in deceitful wiles" (Ephesians 4:14).

To combat cults on the one hand and to break free from the encrustations of denominational traditions on the other, thousands of churches have joined a back-to-the-Bible movement. They are reacting to the conflicting claims of religious leaders in the spirit of the Bereans of Acts 17:11:

> Now these Jews were more noble than those in Thessalonica, for they received the word with all eagerness, examining the scriptures daily to see if these things were so.

The Bereans had listened as Paul labored to persuade them that Jesus of Nazareth was indeed the promised Messiah. Paul's claims were so radical, however, that the Bereans refused to accept them at first hearing. Before they could believe, they had to be certain that his report was in harmony with the standard of truth, the Scriptures. Only then would they receive his teaching. They were using the Scriptures exactly as today's New Testament church does, as the authoritative guide to the truth.

The Bereans did what Paul later advised Timothy to do (2 Timothy 3). Timothy's society resembled our own with its declining morals, empty and fanatical religions, and rampant false teaching. Paul reminded him that in the Scriptures Timothy had all he needed to protect himself and his church from error. So convinced was Paul of the Scriptures' truth, he had willingly suffered persecution rather than swerve from it. Knowing by experience what temptations would confront Timothy in his ministry, the older man encouraged him to "continue in what you have learned and firmly believed," remembering the teaching he had received from his mother Eunice and his grandmother Lois and his other mentors in the faith. Hold fast to the Scriptures, Paul advised him, for nothing else is needed to guide your churches.

To call the Scriptures "inspired," as Paul does, is to set them apart from all other writings because they are "God-breathed." For centuries Christians have called these inspired writings the Word of God. While the Bible never uses that title for itself, it does employ the term when referring to God's message to the prophets and apostles. The incarnate Lord is also called the Word (John 1). Since the Bible records God's Word to the apostles and prophets and His Word to us in the flesh, it is reasonable to refer to the entire Book as God's Word.

God inspired the apostles and prophets to speak (John 16:13; 1 Corinthians 12:2, 3) their messages were called the Word of God (1 Thessalonians 2:13). What they spoke and wrote became the foundation of the church (Ephesians 2:20). The earliest Christians verified that they spoke the truth, because many of them lived through the events they described and could personally testify that what the apostles declared really happened (1 Corinthians 15:1-6).

God has protected His Word through the centuries that separate us from Christianity's early days. The Dead Sea Scroll discovery in 1947, for example, has added evidence of reliability of the Old Testament. Of the approximately 5000 manuscripts we have with all or parts of the New Testament on them, we can test the faithfulness of the copies. What we have learned is fascinating. William Barclay states that there are approximately 150,000 places in which there are variant readings among the manuscripts, often only a difference in spelling or word order, or a substitute of one synonym for another. Actually less than 400 of the variations affect the sense, and of these fewer than 50 are important differences. And in no case is an article of faith or a precept of duty left in any doubt.

The twentieth-century church can be confident, therefore, that it has a reliable record of the early church's practices and of God's will for His people.

It would be a little more accurate for the twentieth-century church to refer to itself as an apostolic church, rather than a Bible church. The New Testament, rather than the entire Bible, is the norm of faith and practice for the church. It is the foundation of the church because it contains the record of Christianity's days of creation and development, days in which the apostles taught the infant churches and guided them in the truth. The apostles had been with Jesus; they had been especially commissioned by Him to make disciples; they knew the mind of Christ and were aided in their memory by the Holy Spirit. Only through them, in fact, do we have any record of Christ's ministry and passion. The church from the beginning has been dependent upon their teaching as recorded in the New Testament.

This does not mean that the New Testament church is anti-Old Testament. To the contrary, the early churches accepted the Old Testament as Scripture; they had no others until the books that became the New Testament were circulated and eventually canonized. The New Testament cannot even be fully understood apart from the Old. Since the New Covenant is the fulfillment of the Old, however, the documents of the older covenant do not have the binding power upon Christians that the documents of the New (New Testament) have.

We are an apostolic church in the sense defined by Tertullian about the year A.D. 200:

> Hence then the ruling which we lay down; that since Jesus Christ sent out the Apostles to preach, no others are to be accepted as preachers but those whom Christ appointed . . . Now the substance of their preaching, that is, Christ's revelation to them, must be approved, on my ruling, only through the testimony of those churches which the Apostles founded by preaching to them both *viva voce* and afterwards by their letters. If this is so, it is likewise clear that all doctrine which accords with these apostolic churches, the sources and origins of the faith, must be reckoned as truth, since it maintains without doubt what the churches received from the Apostles, the Apostles from Christ, and Christ from God. . . . We are in communion with the apostolic churches because there is no difference of doctrine. This is our guarantee of truth.

In our emphasis upon the importance of the Bible for today's church, we must include this warning: To be a Bible church is not to worship the Bible. While we take the whole Book seriously, we do so because it provides all the information available about the One whom we worship and the church He established. Life is to be found in Him, not in the Book:

> You search the scriptures, because you think that in them you have eternal life; and it is they that bear witness to me; yet you refuse to come to me that you may have life (John 5:39, 40).

Jesus himself thus warns against bibliolatry; we are not to worship the Book but the Lord of the Book.

With this warning in mind, we can now assert that the Scriptures are highly treasured by Christians, who agree with Paul that they are "profitable. . . ." A closer look at 2 Timothy 3:16, 17 demonstrates their profitability.

For Teaching

Filled with history, poetry, drama, prophecy, and biography, the Scriptures are a library of knowledge. The Christian turns to them initially, however, for a specific purpose: he wants to know about Jesus, the Messiah and Lord of life. The four Gospels do not record everything we should like to know about Him, because they are not written as biographies; instead, "these are written that you may believe that Jesus is the Christ, the Son of God, and that believing you may have life in his name" (John 20:31). The "sacred writings . . . are able to instruct you for salvation through faith in Christ Jesus" (2 Timothy 3:15). Timothy is instructed to "preach the word" from the Scriptures because "the time is coming [and now is] when people will not endure sound teaching, but having itching ears they will accumulate for themselves teachers to suit their own likings, and will turn away from listening to the truth and wander into myths" (2 Timothy 4:1-4).

The Scriptures fulfill their stated purpose. They include all we need to know for salvation and everything that is essential to the establishing of the church. Through the inspired instructions of the Bible one can protect himself from the Jimmie Joneses of today, the latter-day prophets with their latest revelations; we need no high priests or low priests, no new cults or respectable sects to teach us a better way. The way is already available; the Scriptures are profitable for instructing without any other intermediary.

Leslie Weatherhead tells one of many stories that can prove the validity of Paul's words to Timothy. He speaks of the chairman of the missionary meeting in England who claimed to be the founder of a flourishing Christian community in India, although he had never been there himself. When he was five, he said, he had wanted to give a penny to missionaries but he objected to putting his treasure in the impersonal brown box, because there was no proof that his money would get to the mission field. His minister had a friend who was an Indian missionary, so the minister sold the boy a copy of a New Testament for his penny, told him how to mail it to India, and wrote in the flyleaf an inscription giving the name of the boy. When he received the package the missionary in turn gave the Testament to a poor native Indian who had walked many miles to procure one. Twenty years passed. Another missionary was then preaching in a village to people whom he thought had never heard the gospel. As he spoke he noted their excitement. When he paused in his preaching for the question time, he learned that the people there knew Christ and many were serving Him. A little Christian community had been born through the love and life of the native to whom the New Testament had been given. Through its pages the man instructed the people concerning faith and salvation. Although he had no formal education, all he needed was in the Scriptures. He found the New Testament "profitable for teaching."

For Reproof, Correction, and Training in Righteousness

The Scriptures have the power to convict of sin, to correct error, and to enable one to live right before God. No one who reads the Word honestly can escape its cutting, judging, restorative power.

> The word of God is living and active, sharper than any two-edged sword, piercing to the division of soul and spirit, of joints and marrow, and discerning the thoughts and intentions of the heart. And before him no creature is hidden, but all are open and laid bare to the eyes of him with whom we have to do (Hebrews 4:12, 13).

> If any one hears my sayings and does not keep them, I do not judge him; for I did not come to judge the world but to save the world. He

who rejects me and does not receive my sayings has a judge; *the word that I have spoken will be his judge* on the last day (John 12:47, 48).

If you continue in my word, you are truly my disciples, and you will know the truth, and the truth will make you free (John 8:31, 32).

The written Word is all that is needed to convince us of our wayward actions and to correct our mistaken impressions, theories, theologies, and false teachings of every kind. Through the teachings of the Word men and women can be restored to their true humanity, churches can be rebuilt upon their intended foundation.

Many Christians would gladly testify to the changes wrought in their lives once they began to study their Scriptures seriously. They have experienced new peace, highest ethical standards, the assurance of their salvation, and deeper relationships with other Christians.

William Barclay narrates many conversion stories which demonstrate the power of the Scriptures. Here is one of them. A New York gangster was released from prison. On the way to rejoin his old gang, he picked a man's pocket on Fifth Avenue, then slipped into Central Park to see what he had filched. He must have been disappointed when what he thought was a wallet turned out to be a pocket New Testament. Since he had some time before he was expected to meet his gang, he began thumbing through the Testament. Before long he was deeply involved in his reading. A few hours later he went to meet his comrades, but not to join them. He broke with them and with crime. He had discovered the truth, and it had set him free.

Through the Word, then, "the man of God may be complete, equipped for every good work." This sentence refers specifically to those of Timothy's calling, of course. The point is clear: the leaders of the church need nothing more to guide them than the Scriptures; they are sufficient to prepare church leaders to be faithful in every essential detail to the will of the Founder.

What the Church Claims About the Bible

By its reliance upon the authority of the Scriptures, the New Testament church today makes several claims for the Bible.

1. *The Bible is understandable.* It is written in language that can be comprehended by an intelligent reader. One does not

have to hold a seminary degree or be an ordained clergyman to grasp the meaning of the Bible. Most of the New Testament was written in *koine* Greek, the common language of the day. The writers' purpose was to communicate, not to impress. The Scriptures are reasonable, appealing to the mind and expecting to be understood.

2. *The Bible is historical.* The Bible did not appear out of nowhere as a "holy book." Its people actually lived, its towns really existed, the historical events recorded there can be tested against secular history. Unlike the so-called holy books of many cults, the Bible has passed the tests of historicity.

The Christian religion is an historical faith. Its principle teachings are rooted and demonstrated in actual events that took place in time and space with real historical persons. Theological doctrines like the incarnation of God, salvation of man from sin, and resurrection from the dead, for example, are made actual in Jesus. He was born of a virgin, conceived of the Spirit of God. He died on a cross, the final sacrifice for man's sins. He rose from the dead, breaking the grip of death. The Bible does not wrestle philosophically with the nature of God; instead it narrates the events of history through which God has revealed himself.

3. *It can speak for itself.* In fairness to the Bible, Scriptural names should be used for Scriptural truths. Many speculative arguments about the trinity could be resolved, for example, by simply pointing out that the term *trinity* is an abstract philosophical term quite proper to a university classroom but alien to the mind set of the Biblical writers. Arguments over the mode of baptism could quickly be resolved by agreeing to define the word as the Biblical writers did, as dipping, plunging, or immersing. Denominational partisanship could be lessened by agreeing to call no church after any human personality or system and simply to use names that are Biblical names.

4. *It is purposeful.* What John said of his Gospel ("these are written that you may believe"), he could have said of the entire New Testament. Even the very important book of Acts, which is the history of the church's origins, is more than history. It is a highly selective record of the expansion of the early church, delineating a conversion theology that can guide subsequent centuries in winning people to Christ and forming them into churches. The epistles deal with the nature of faith and the

Christian life within the community of believers. Revelation assures threatened Christians that they are secure because their faith is in the Lord of history. Taken together, the New Testament books testify to the importance of the church, the simplicity of the faith, and the necessity for trust in Christ. For 2,000 years the Scriptures have guided the church, when they have been available to Christians. When the church has divided or strayed from the truth, it has not been the fault of the guide.

5. *It deserves to be read critically.* Bible students have no need to fear subjecting the Bible to the same standards of judgment they would use when reading any other historical or literary work. Because the Bible was written over hundreds of years by dozens of authors, each individual book must be read in the light of

its historical setting

the author's individual personality

his reason for writing

the audience to whom he was writing

and whether he is speaking a particular truth

for a specific audience or a universal truth

for all people of all time.

By these criteria we know that the book of Esther does not have the relevance for today's church that the book of Acts can claim. Commandments which are specifically for the people of God under the Mosaic covenant are not as binding upon today's Christians as Christ's commandments under the New Covenant. When the writer of Hebrews declares that "in many and various ways God spoke of old to our fathers by the prophets; but in these last days he has spoken to us by a Son," he is contrasting the old and the new messages from God. The whole of Hebrews expands upon this contrast and glories in the difference. The same God who spoke originally through the prophets has now spoken with finality and power through His Son. His direct instructions require close attention; wherever He supersedes the prophets, we follow the Son.

A Bible church rests upon the inspired, authoritative Scriptures as sufficient rule in faith and order. This does not mean that a twentieth-century church can afford to ignore the intervening 2,000 years of church history. Not at all. We are indebted to Christian giants in every generation for their contribution to the church. Today's Christian inherits the legacy of

Augustine, Aquinas, Luther, Calvin, Knox, John and Charles Wesley, Campbell, and a whole host of heroes of the faith. But our ultimate allegiance is not to any man or agency, but to Jesus Christ. There is only one Book that we can trust without reservation to teach us about Him and His church. That Book is the Bible.

For Further Consideration

1. How can a full knowledge of the Bible combat the hold of cults on the one hand and denominational traditions on the other?
2. What does *inspired* mean?
3. How can we claim that New Testament churches today can be guided by the same writings that guided the church in Timothy's day?
4. Can the apostolic church really exist in the twentieth century?
5. What warning did Jesus issue regarding the Scriptures?
6. In addition to the Scriptures, what do we need to know for salvation and for establishing churches?
7. Many Christians confess that they don't read the Bible because it is too difficult to comprehend. Yet this chapter claims that the Bible is quite understandable. What do you think?
8. What does the above question suggest about the value of modern translations?
9. What is the purpose of the Bible?
10. What are some good questions to ask when reading the Bible?

CHAPTER SEVEN

The Church
At Worship

(Revelation 5:1-14)

In a famous broadcast to the United States, England's Arch-bishop William Temple made what he knew could be called an outrageous statement. "This world can be saved from political chaos and collapse by one thing only," he announced, "and that is worship."

For to worship is to quicken the conscience by the holiness of God, to feed the mind with the truth of God, to purge the imagination by the beauty of God, to open the heart to the love of God, to devote the will to the purpose of God.

We would like to agree with Temple that worldwide worship would lead to worldwide peace. It is difficult to do so, however, since the earth is already covered with monuments of man's worship, some of which (like Jerusalem's beleaguered Wailing Wall or, for that matter, the holy city itself) are contested prizes in bloody holy wars. There is no lack of worship in this world. Japanese visit their myriads of Shinto shrines, Indians their plentiful Hindu temples, Muslims their Mecca and Jews their promised land. It was an exaggerated expression of worship that cost Jimmie Jones' fanatical followers their lives in Guyana.

In America, growing religious bodies like Mormons or Jehovah's Witnesses can depend on the righteous zeal of their adherents to expand their cause; smaller but equally zealous groups like the Amish and the followers of Reverend Moon are devoted to their form of worship. Bizarre cultists annually gather for their Pan Pagan Festival, a conclave of occultists and witches. There is no lack of worship on this globe.

Yet the Archbishop was not wrong to call for worship, especially as he defines it. He wants to improve the souls and behavior of humanity. Worship will do that, if the object of one's worship is the true God and the manner of worshiping is harmonious with God's will. Such devotion can indeed unite mankind and produce peace.

The Bible is outspoken, however, in defining the purpose of worship to be less in what is done for us than what we do for God. The disappointed church member who complains that he is not getting much out of the church's worship services betrays his self-centeredness; he has made himself the object of worship by expecting the church to elevate or entertain him. He treats himself as God, the idol of his own adoration. He would benefit from the counsel of a wise Christian leader who said, "My friend, it makes very little difference what you get out of it. What is important in worship is what God gets out of it; it is Him you are worshiping, not yourself."

Willard Sperry recounts the incident in his *Reality and Worship* of the Boston minister who was visiting his Catholic friend. As the Roman Catholic showed his Protestant companion through the church they came in time into a dim recess behind the great organ, where in a bare, dark spot a lay brother was on his hands and knees scrubbing the floor. When the visitor exclaimed that surely no one would ever see this hidden place, the man on his knees quickly retorted, "No, no one ever comes in here. We keep this place clean for the eye of God." The lay brother understood the meaning of worship.

Our English word *worship* derives from the old Saxon *weorthscipe* (worth-ship), which means ascribing worth or value to someone because we consider him worthy of homage or reverence. The lay brother was scrubbing the floor because God is worthy of such homage, whether any human eyes could see the floor or not. Paul uses precisely this sense of God's worth in his exhortation to slaves:

> Slaves, be obedient to those who are your earthly masters, with fear and trembling, in singleness of heart, *as to Christ;* not in the way

of eyeservice, as men-pleasers, but as *servants of Christ,* doing the will of God from the heart, rendering service with a good will *as to the Lord and not to men* (Ephesians 6:5-7).

In John's vision of heavenly worship (Revelation 5:1-14), the essential nature of earthly adoration of God is presented. Here is the triumphant Lord, who, having vanquished all other gods, reigns high and lifted up on His throne. Surrounding Him are the twenty-four elders and four beasts who represent all peoples and history. His hand holds the scroll upon which is written His universal plan for the destiny of the world. No one can reveal what is written on the scroll; its secret is locked up against all except the One who is worthy to reveal it.

"Who is worthy?" an angel loudly asks. There is none except One: only the Lion of the tribe of Judah, the Root of David, the Lamb who was slain (that is, Jesus Christ) is worthy to reveal God's plan to men, for He is their conquering Savior. He alone responds to the question. As He moves, the elders and creatures fall down in praise; all history kneels before Him. "*Worthy* art thou to take the scroll," they sing in worship.

We can clarify the meaning of *worship* by thinking of a television commercial that has profaned its meaning. A beautiful, voluptuous woman appears on the screen selling L'Oreal products. She boasts that this line of cosmetics is terribly expensive but, she adds, "I'm worth it." She is willing to pay whatever the cost because of her worth. She does not realize it, but the young lady is making a religious statement, announcing her scale of values and priorities.

The Ten Commandments open with an injunction to acknowledge the ultimate worth of God: "You shall have no other gods before me." Only He is worthy! When Jesus was asked to name the greatest commandment, His answer began, "You shall love the Lord your God with all your heart, and with all your soul, and with all your mind" (Matthew 22:37). You shall treat Him as worthy of receiving all you have to give, of having first place in your scale of priorities. Under the law of Moses, the Israelites expressed their sense of God's worth through community worship, tithes and offerings, support of their priesthood, and observance of the Sabbath. They brought up their children to revere Him. He was worthy. In the New Covenant, Christ shares that worth and is placed above all dominions, powers, and principalities. Every knee shall bow before Him (Philippians 2:5-11).

One's god, then, is whatever he finds worthy of his total allegiance, whatever he is willing to sacrifice everything else in order to preserve and honor. We have no choice in the matter: We cannot live without an established order of values. Whether we can easily explain our faith or not, we daily make decisions based on this scale of priorities. Whatever is first on the list is our god, whether that be self, or sex, or money, or fame, or family, or Jesus Christ. "Man must and will have some religion," William Blake asserted. "If he has not the religion of Jesus, he will have the religion of Satan, and will erect the synagogue of Satan, calling the Prince of this World 'God,' and destroying all who do not worship Satan under the name of God . . ." Although Blake wrote nearly 200 years ago, the rise of the occult, including Satan worship, in the twentieth century gives weight to his prophetic words. Man will worship. The only question is, Whom will it be? Who is worthy?

The Biblical answer is unequivocal:

> Worthy is the Lamb who was slain, to receive power and wealth and wisdom and might and honor and glory and blessing! . . . To him who sits upon the throne and to the Lamb be blessing and honor and glory and might for ever and ever! (Revelation 5:12, 13)

Whatever we do for Him is our worship. Since His Word has left a record of how those who knew Christ best expressed their love for Him, it seems only reasonable that we who love Him also would imitate them in doing what they knew would please Him. Worship is doing everything in our power to please God from whom all blessings flow.

In both the Old and the New Testaments, worship has the double meaning of serving and of prostrating oneself. One worships by *kneeling* before the Lord; one also worships by *serving* Him. In its community form, Old Testament worship involved sacrifices, ritual purifications of the body with accompanying changes of clothing, offerings of drink and oil, and the required tithes. Prominent in worship were all kinds of music, including solos, anthems, shoutings, dancing, and processions. Receiving the Word of the Lord in oracles, from prophets and in the study of Scripture, was also considered worship. A balance

71

to the somewhat noisy adoration of God was encouraged in the practice of silent meditation. In all these forms, the purpose was not self-improvement but the offering of praise due the God of Abraham, Isaac, and Jacob.

In the New Testament, the corporate worship of the church leaned heavily on Jewish antecedents. The early Christians continued many familiar practices from the synagogue, but imbued the Jewish forms with peculiarly Christian meanings. They continued public prayers, but they now prayed in Jesus' name. They still sang their psalms, but with new meaning since the foretold Messiah had come. The Scriptures were studied as before in the synagogue, but the Christians concentrated their studies on the life and expectations of Christ, and after several years the lives of Jesus (Gospels) and the circulating letters of the apostles were added to the Old Testament books. Most significantly, the annual Passover meal was replaced by the weekly Lord's Supper.

Christians did not slavishly imitate the synagogue, however. The new Christian faith was an outpouring of the Spirit of God that would not be confined to any previously set limits. The new wine could not be kept in old wineskins. Such new or newly vital ideas as the personal fatherhood of God, the personal saviorhood of Christ, the promise of one's own resurrection from the dead, and the forgiveness of one's personal sins forever, the new life in Christ—these demanded expressions in worship.

Revelation 5 includes many of the aspects of public worship. Praising God with prayer and song dominates the passage. In Ephesians 5:18, 19 Paul exhorts Christians,

> Do not get drunk with wine, for that is debauchery; but be filled with the Spirit, addressing one another in psalms and hymns and spiritual songs, singing and making melody to the Lord with all your heart.

Music occupies an important position in Christian worship, for Christian faith pours itself out in laughter and singing. In the earliest churches, the chants and music were practically identical with the customs of the synagogue. Little is explicitly said concerning music in the churches in the New Testament, but in Revelation both vocal and instrumental music are afforded an exalted role, one similar to their honored places in modern church services.

We have already studied the place of teaching, fellowship, the breaking of bread, and the prayers in the early church (Acts 2:42). All these worship expressions centered on Christ. When you love someone, you never hear enough about him. Those earliest Christians assembled with the implicit request, "Tell us more about Jesus." I recently lost a very dear friend in a tragic airplane crash. Since then, whenever her other friends and I happen to meet, we inevitably share our insights and stories about her. We loved her unique personality and varied abilities. We can't help talking about her. She's worth it.

That same impulse drew the early Christians together. They wanted to learn more about Jesus and to be together with His other friends. They never grew bored with praising Him any more than we tire of recalling and rediscovering a beloved friend.

Toward the end of a Holy Land tour I asked the group to recall the highlight of the trip. Almost unanimously the members agreed that our Communion service in the upper room was the most moving moment of the entire trip. There we sang hymns in the room's natural sound chamber that transformed our little group into a great choir; there we partook of the bread and wine and meditated upon Christ's incredible sacrifice. We prayed together and felt our souls reaching out to one another and toward God. We assumed the role of first-century Christians extolling the worth of Christ.

By the second century, incidentally, a change had taken place. Pliny, the governor of Bithynia, in his letter to the emperor Trajan (A.D. 113) describes Christian worship:

> They were accustomed on a special day to assemble before day-light and to sing antiphonally a hymn to Christ as if he were a god, and to bind themselves by an oath not for any wrong purpose, but not to commit theft or robbery or adultery, not to break their word or to deny a deposit when asked for. After this it was their custom to depart, and to meet together again to take food, but ordinary and harmless food.

Apparently two separate services were held on their special day (probably Sunday). We note the importance of their common meal.

By the middle of the second century, Christian worship had adopted a formula with which we are still familiar. Justin Martyr indicates that Sunday is the special day for a service that begins with the reading of Scriptures (the Greek Old Testament and the Gospels) and continues with a sermon (delivered by the president of the assembly, who is seated in his chair in the customary way of teaching for that day) and common prayers. Then follows a kiss of peace and the offertory of bread and wine, which the deacons arrange on the table before the bishop. The bishop then offers a consecration prayer and the deacons serve the Communion. The common meal with the special service of bread and wine, which marked the earliest Christian gatherings, had by a century later become the more formal worship service with the Lord's Supper as the climactic act of reverence. It is not easy to retain the spontaneity and power of the New Testament churches; it was inevitable that the informality of the earliest days of the faith would give way to a more structured worship.

Prayers are such a neutral manner of worship we tend to take them for granted. The earliest Christians prayed in the temple and in their Christian house church meetings, as well as individually. They had a new motive and mediator in their prayers, since they now accepted Christ as their high priest and intercessor with God, but they who had always prayed to God continued with a heightened sense of gratitude for what God had given them in Christ.

The Scriptures record that "fear came upon every soul" (Acts 2). They lived constantly with the reality of God's outpouring of His power in their minds. Theirs was no casual "Sunday-go-to-meeting" religion. They revered the Lord. Worship was a community experience but it was also a constant personal daily practice. It is therefore no surprise that "many wonders and signs were done through the apostles." The Holy Spirit had descended and empowered the church's appointed leaders. God was obviously at work among them. Luke wrote the Acts of the Apostles to record the Spirit's amazing activities as He paved the way for the preaching of the gospel and the planting of new churches. Christians saw daily evidence of the Spirit's accomplishments. They felt they had every reason to praise the Lord.

At first the Christians met daily (Acts 2), but before the New

Testament era had come to a close, daily community worship had yielded to one special day a week. That day was no longer the Sabbath, which the Jews had observed in honor of the exodus from Egypt, but the first day of the week in recognition of Christ's history-changing return from the grave. Christians have always called Sunday the Lord's Day. It has never been the Sabbath, but the day of resurrection. It was so important that when Constantine, the first Roman emperor to embrace Christianity ascended his throne (in the fourth century), he ordered his armies to have special devotional services on Sunday and declared that no courts were to be held and no public shows, theaters, dancing, or amusements to be allowed to profane the Lord's Day. Even earlier the church father Tertullian observed, "A true Christian, according to the commands of the gospel, observes the Lord's Day by casting out all bad thoughts, and cherishing all goodness, honoring the resurrection of the Lord, which took place on that day." In addition to the expected purposes of worship, the Scriptures specifically state that the gathering was in order to break bread (Acts 20:7) and to encourage one another (Hebrews 10:23-25).

In secular America, the Lord's Day has lost much of its meaning even for Christians. It is undoubtedly good that civil law no longer requires all citizens to observe the day; legislated worship is not worship at all. It is also helpful to true Christian worship that attendance at worship no longer advances one's social status or chances for political achievement. There can finally be only one reason to observe the Lord's Day, one reason to forsake the tempting allurements of recreation or sloth: God is worth a special day.

In his *Return to Religion,* psychiatrist Henry C. Link explains why he returned to church attendance after several years' absence. He says he goes for reasons most of us would give for staying home: he would rather linger in bed on Sunday mornings and read the Sunday papers. Although he knows his father and parents-in-law will be pleased if he goes, and that he's setting a good example for his children, he also knows that he'll have to shake hands with people he doesn't care about and he might be asked to do something he would rather not do. He'll probably disagree with the sermon, and his friends—who know the truth about him—will consider him a hypocrite. Furthermore, he doesn't agree with all the doctrines of his church or any other church. He concludes by admitting that he hates to go but he knows it will do him good.

Dr. Link touches on many motives for worship: personal discipline, desire to please others whose approval is important, need for social intercourse with others beyond one's peers and friends, need to set a good example for one's children, belief that children should be taught the values for which the church stands, challenge to try the unexpected or even unwanted, stimulus to intellectual dialogue. These are admirable goals that attendance at the church's public meetings will fulfill, but they miss the real purpose of worship. What is at stake, as we asserted early in this chapter, is not the benefit of worship to the believer but the believer's praise of God. Above all else, we submit to the rigors of Christian worship because Christ is worth it.

Worthy is the Lamb . . .

For Further Consideration

1. What is the real purpose of worship?
2. Define *worship*.
3. If a person's god is whatever he places first in his life, what is the leading god in our country? (There may be more than one.)
4. What are the two kinds of worship discussed here?
5. How did the Jewish synagogue influence formal Christian worship?
6. What changes in Christian worship can we see between the first and second centuries?
7. Why did the Christians change the special day of worship from Saturday to Sunday?
8. How important is the observing of the Lord's Day in a Christian's worship?

CHAPTER EIGHT

The Church
At Communion

(1 Corinthians 11:23-26)

When Jesus ate the last supper in the upper room with His disciples, it was not an entirely unusual event for them. They had eaten many such meals together. What made this common meal different, however, was Jesus' foreknowledge of what was about to happen to Him. From the upper room He would go to the Garden of Gethsemane, there to agonize over His appointed destiny. Then would come His humiliation before the Jewish court and Pilate. Then the cross.

From the moment the newest Christians began meeting together following their Pentecost experience, therefore, it was inevitable that they would remember that last supper. They would do so because Jesus had always enjoined His followers to eat together; they would also do so because they wanted especially to remember that last night when He had said, "This is my body . . . this is my blood . . . for you." Such events as the risen Christ's appearance to the two at Emmaus, where He was not recognized until He had broken bread with them (Luke 24:30f), and His eating with them in Jerusalem (Acts 1:4) reinforced their desire to make the common meal the central expression of their fellowship. When Christians meet at the Lord's table we are participating in a *living memorial to Christ*. We are there to remember. "Do this in remembrance of me," Jesus said of the bread and cup (1 Corinthians 11:24).

When the fabulously wealthy American businessman Howard Hughes died a few years ago, he was honored in Las Vegas in a remarkably callous way. For sixty seconds the pit bosses held their dice at crap tables; the roulette wheels were stilled, the casinos quiet. Then a man at Desert Inn yelled, "OK, he had his minute. Let's deal 'em." Hughes had amassed a fantastic fortune in his heyday. He indulged his every fantasy and played with the world's most expensive toys, but he had lost touch with men. They gave him what they thought he had coming—sixty seconds of respect. Then he was forgotten.

Jesus, on the other hand, amassed no fortune, owned no properties or playthings, wrote no books, held no political power, depended on his friends for financial support, had no home, earned no academic degrees, and died an apparent failure. But nearly 2000 years later millions of His friends remember Him every week in this simple memorial service. What made the difference? Not just the obvious contrasts mentioned above, but the history-changing difference Christ made, a change in the relationship between God and man, which Jesus mentions as He blesses the cup of wine: "This cup is the *new covenant* in my blood."

His disciples knew immediately what He meant by those words, although they did not fully grasp their implication until after Christ's resurrection. As lifelong Jews they had always believed their God was a covenant-keeping God. Hadn't He called Abraham out of Haran to a new land and hadn't He promised to make of Abraham's descendants a great nation? And hadn't He sealed that promise with the sign of the covenant, circumcision?

When Moses led the Israelites from slavery in Egypt toward freedom in the promised land, a new covenant (agreement, contract) was drawn up between God and His people at Sinai. To seal that agreement, Moses

> rose early in the morning, and built an altar at the foot of the mountain, and twelve pillars, according to the twelve tribes of Israel. And he sent young men of the people of Israel, who offered burnt offerings and sacrificed peace offerings of oxen to the Lord. And Moses took half of the blood and put it in basins, and half of the blood he threw against the altar. Then he took the book of the covenant, and read it in the hearing of the people; and they said, "All that the Lord has spoken we will do, and we will be obedient." And Moses took

the blood and threw it upon the people, and said, "Behold the blood of the covenant which the Lord has made with you in accordance with all these words" (Exodus 24:4-8).

To the Jew, blood was the sacred symbol of life. In throwing the blood upon the altar and then upon the people, Moses was symbolically intermingling God's life and His people's lives. God was giving himself to His people in the blood and they were responding in kind, sealing their promise to be obedient to all that God had spoken to them. God had taken the initiative; He had selected them to be His own. Their blood offering proved their desire to accept His selection. They would have Him to be their God as He would hold them to be His people. It was a contract signed in blood.

When Jesus held the wine before them as a symbol of a new agreement, they could not have known all that was coming, but they did understand that God through Christ was preparing to write a new contract with His people. After they saw the victorious, risen Christ, they recalled Jesus' words. They then realized what was happening on the cross. There Jesus was delivering God's New Covenant to His people. He who was called Son of God and Son of man personally offered the life of man and the life of God upon the altar. There He changed the terms of God's agreement with His people. The cross divided history into an Old Testament period and a New Testament era, with the New Covenant of love and grace supplanting the Old Covenant of law and sacrifice. "He has appeared once for all at the end of the age to put away sin by the sacrifice of himself . . ." (Hebrews 9:26).

The writer of Hebrews explains Jesus' mediation of the new agreement in the following passage:

> When Christ appeared as a high priest of the good things that have come, then through the greater and more perfect tent (not made with hands, that is, not of this creation) he entered once for all into the Holy Place, taking not the blood of goats and calves but his own blood, thus securing an eternal redemption. For if the sprinkling of defiled persons with the blood of goats and bulls and with the ashes of a heifer sanctifies for the purification of the flesh, how much more shall the blood of Christ, who through the eternal Spirit offered himself without blemish to God, purify your conscience from dead works to serve the living God. Therefore he is the mediator of a new covenant . . . (9:11-15).

[Jesus] has no need, like those high priests, to offer sacrifices daily, first for his own sins and then for those of the people; he did this once for all when he offered up himself (7:27).

The Lord's Supper commemorates this supreme sacrifice and the meditation of a New Covenant. As soon as Peter's hearers confessed their faith in Christ and were baptized into Him on the Day of Pentecost, they eagerly sought out one another in order to learn more about Him. They studied the Scriptures concerning Him and gladly heard all the apostles could tell them of His marvelous deeds. But their special moment was when the bread was broken and the wine passed. All their attention was on Christ; they remembered the cross and they celebrated the freedom He bought for them with His blood. Because of His cross, they were slaves to sin and the law no more. He had signed the new agreement with God on their behalf, in blood.

The author of Hebrews again captures the full significance of the Lord's Supper as a memorial when he exhorts his fellow Christians in the following manner:

> Therefore, brethren, since we have confidence to enter the sanctuary by the blood of Jesus [no Jew under the Old Covenant would have dared enter the Holy of Holies in the temple, except the high priest on his appointed yearly visit], by the new and living way which he opened for us through the curtain, that is, through his flesh, and since we have a great priest over the house of God [Christ himself], let us draw near with a true heart in full assurance of faith, with our hearts sprinkled clean [as Moses sprinkled the people with blood at Sinai] from an evil conscience and our bodies washed with pure water [in baptism]. Let us hold fast the confession of our hope without wavering, for he who promised is faithful; and let us consider how to stir up one another to love and good works, not neglecting to meet together, as is the habit of some, but encouraging one another, and all the more as you see the Day drawing near (10:19-25).

As a memorial feast, the Lord's Supper recalls the terms of the New Covenant, which opened the way to God without an earthly priest to mediate on our behalf; it also encourages us to hold fast, to be faithful, and to encourage one another in the Lord. The Lord's table may represent many things to us, but it is always Jesus' appointed way to remember Him.

It is also a *thanksgiving feast*. Before distributing the bread and wine Jesus gave thanks. This was the Jewish custom at the Passover meal and at regular meals. When Christians give thanks for the bread and cup at the Lord's table, we are therefore imitating Jesus—but we are doing far more. We are expressing gratitude for all God has done for us through Christ. This element of the meal was so important to early Christians that in the post-apostolic and later periods the service was called the Eucharist, from the Greek word meaning thanksgiving. It is synonymous with *eulogein,* to bless, the term that usually was employed to translate the Hebrew root for blessings over food. The Lord's Supper is a blessed meal for which we give thanks; it is also the thanksgiving we offer for our blessings.

When a Christian matures in his relationship with God, his most characteristic quality is gratitude. A leading theologian was asked to explain his prayer life, especially to name what he most asked God to give him. He replied, "For the most part I just give thanks." His gratitude had replaced his petitions. For centuries the Lord's Supper has offered Christians a regular, formal means of expressing thanks.

The impulse to give thanks has always been an important motive in a Christian's desire to observe the Lord's Supper frequently. If Acts 2:42 ("the breaking of bread") refers to the ceremony of Communion as well as eating a common meal, the custom of the earliest church was daily Communion. More than two decades later, at Troas (20:7), this service of Communion was apparently a weekly observation, which it has remained since then. At Troas the Communion was enjoyed at night, but by the time of Justin (A.D. 150), Christians were partaking of the bread and wine in the daytime, probably to counteract the anti-Christian rumors that the believers were indulging in shameful nocturnal revelries. The weekly service, whether by night or by day, has always afforded Christians an opportunity to praise God and give thanks.

"How sharper than a serpent's tooth it is to have a thankless child," Shakespeare's King Lear moaned. Aware of how easily we take Christ for granted and accept God's blessings as somehow our right instead of God's grace, Christians who have made a practice of faithful weekly attendance at the Lord's table, though they may never use the churchly term *Eucharist,* look forward to each Sunday as a special occasion to give thanks and praise to the One from whom all blessings flow.

The most common term for the Lord's Supper is *Communion*. We have met this word before as *fellowship*. The root means sharing and is translated variously as communion, fellowship, common, communication, participation, partnership, and so on. It signifies *to hold in common*. From the beginning, Communion has been a common or shared meal. When Christians were still meeting in one another's homes, they carried food to their gatherings. In addition to the study, prayer, and praise time, they enjoyed eating together, helping themselves to what everyone contributed to the meal. These love feasts (*agape* meals) expressed as almost nothing else could their acceptance of one another as equals before Christ. Here Christian could share with Christian regardless of cultural, economic, social, or previous religious differences. They were one. This fact explains Paul's consternation when the meal was being abused by Corinthian Christians, whose quarrels and selfishness made it impossible for them to eat in fellowship with one another. They could not celebrate the memorial of *one body* and give thanks for their unity in Christ in their fractious, divided condition.

It is enlightening to reflect on the importance of meals in Jesus' ministry. As baptism was the sign for John the Baptist, meals could almost be adopted as a sign of Jesus' ministry. We picture John at the Jordan, dressed in his camel's hair garment, baptizing the repentant Jews who came to him, but remaining a loner, subsisting on locusts and wild honey, a separated prophet calling his people to repentance. Jesus, on the other hand, had to wrest himself away from the crowds that thronged to Him. His periods of solitude are all the more noteworthy because He was usually surrounded by people. Unlike John, He entered readily into social intercourse. His meals were taken with His companions, and many of their most cherished memories recalled events at meals, from the feeding of the 5,000 to the quiet repasts at the home of Mary and Martha or Simon the Pharisee, or even their plucking ears of grain on the Sabbath, unfortunately, and His defense of their action. Their most memorable meal, of course, was the one they had with Him in the upper room on the night He was betrayed. They recalled His broad hints of impending doom, His humble act of washing their feet, His heartbroken revelation that one who was eating with them would betray Him, their singing and simple enjoyment in being together.

Later they would identify their sharing in the Communion as an expression of their actual partnership in Christ's cause and death: "The cup of blessing which we bless, is it not a participation in the blood of Christ?" (1 Corinthians 10:16) In the act of communing Christians renew their loyalty to Christ and their identification with His cause.

Buzz Aldrin sensed something of this meaning. One of the first two men on the moon, Aldrin took along two little plastic packages containing bread and wine. Just before he partook of the elements (the wine being the first liquid poured and the bread the first food eaten on the moon) he read John 15:5 to indicate the adventurers' trust: "I am the vine, you are the branches. He who abides in me, and I in him, he it is that bears much fruit." The wine of Communion, of which Jesus said, "This is my blood," commingles with the blood of the participant as the sap of the vine flows through the branches, the one participating in the other. Such is the intimacy of the believer with his Lord.

Communion also represents our sharing with one another in Christ. This is the context of 1 Corinthians 11. The Corinthian Christians were faithful enough in observing Communion, but if they remembered its meaning relative to Christ they forgot that it also symbolizes Christian sharing. Where Communion represents unity, they were divided; where it calls us to sober reflection of our obligation to our fellow Christians, some were rudely eating and drinking to excess while others were being ignored; where its very sacredness calls for serious devotion, some were turning the celebration into a raucous party and were even getting drunk on the wine. To partake in this thoughtless way is to invite the Scriptural scolding for doing so in "an unworthy manner," thus "profaning the body and blood of the Lord" (11:27).

The social aspect of Communion is sometimes not fully appreciated. The Lord's Supper was never intended as a mass in which the individual worshiper attends and receives the wafer directly from a priest without regard to fellow participants. Nor should it be profaned as an Arizona company recently has done, advertising individually wrapped communion wafers and grape juice for mail-order use by religious radio and television shows. *Communion* by definition demands participation; it is a meal.

Most churches now use individual Communion cups, a compromise with the dictates of modern hygiene. When a debate was held by the Lutheran ministerium of Pennsylvania in 1895 to decide whether to use the same cup for everyone or individual cups for each member, one person argued for the single cup while encouraging concern about others: "Instead of changing Christ's ordinance, sweeping mustaches should be clipped and those who drink, smoke, chew tobacco, or rub snuff should refrain so as not to foul the sacred cup." Although separate cups for each member has become customary, we can hope that the meaning of the *one* cup and the *one* loaf has not been lost; we partake of the Lord's Supper with reverence for Christ and with thoughtful respect for one another.

One more aspect of Communion must be noted here. In addition to its being a memorial feast, a thanksgiving feast, and a common meal, it is certainly *a celebration of hope*. "For as often as you eat this bread and drink the cup, you proclaim the Lord's death *until he comes*," Paul writes in 1 Corinthians 11:26. The Lord's Supper thus not only recalls the past (Christ's sacrificial death on the cross following the final meal in the upper room) and unifies the present (by our renewing of allegiance to Christ and fellowship with one another in Him), but it turns the Christian's eye to Christ's victorious return and final fulfillment of God's plans for this earth. It testifies that the Christ who died is alive; therefore we who have died with Him and are alive in Him anticipate a resurrection like His. Like Paul we "press on toward the goal for the prize of the upward call of God in Christ Jesus" (Philippians 3:14). Each time we come to His table we eat like pilgrims on the way to our heavenly destiny, never certain but that this might be the last meal before He comes to meet us with the good news that the journey is over.

For Further Consideration

1. As a memorial service, what does the Lord's Supper help us remember?
2. What is the "new covenant" to which Jesus refers as He gives His disciples the cup of wine?
3. What is the importance of *blood* in the Bible?
4. As a thanksgiving feast, for what does the Lord's Supper encourage us to give thanks?

5. Why is gratitude so central in Christian devotion?
6. As a Communion service, what does the Lord's Supper teach us that we have in common with Christ and with other Christians?
7. Can one really partake of the Lord's Supper alone?
8. Although this chapter does not discuss the question specifically, what does it suggest about the relationship between church membership and Communion?
9. As a celebration of hope, what does Communion encourage us to anticipate?

CHAPTER NINE

The Church
That Shares

(Acts 2:42-47; 2 Corinthians 8:1-5)

We have no difficulty understanding that the earliest Christians devoted themselves to "the apostle's teaching . . . the breaking of bread and the prayers," but we stumble over their devotion to *fellowship*. We have so cheapened the meaning of this rich word that in some circles to mention it is to think of coffee and cookies ("Please remain following the service for our fellowship hour"). Yet no one imagines that it was to coffee and cookies that the earliest Christians devoted themselves.

Fellowship is only one of several possible translations for the Greek *koinonia*, the verb form of which means basically to have in common or to share. From that simple definition, as we noted in the last chapter, come such related English words as association, Communion, fellowship, participation, partnership, and generosity. It can refer to the concrete proof of that fellow-feeling, such as a gift or contribution. The new Christians were devoting themselves to the shared life they were now experiencing in Christ and with *fellow* Christians. When they received Christ into their lives they evidenced their new faith by being baptized *into* Christ, then sharing their lives fully with Him ("It is no longer I who live but Christ who lives in me") and, consequently, with one another (they "had all things in common"). As we saw in Chapter 8, the Communion service dramatizes the believers' shared life in Christ:

The cup of blessing which we bless, is it not a participation [fellowship] in the blood of Christ? The bread which we break, is it not a participation [fellowship] in the body of Christ? (1 Corinthians 10:16)

When we participate in the Communion service, we recall that we were joined to Christ in baptism, volunteering to take our part in His sacrificial death. He and we have been united in death and life (Romans 6:1-11). The Communion further demonstrates our fellowship with one another: together at one table, we drink of one cup and eat of one loaf. We are *fellow* members of the body of Christ.

Fundamentally, then, fellowship means sharing. To be in fellowship with Christ is to share our lives with Him as He shares himself with us; to be in fellowship with one another in Christ is to generously give to and take from one another. When we received the "right hand of fellowship" (Galatians 2:9) upon our entrance into the church, we were accepted as full participants in the total ministry of the body. From that moment we have been living in the protective presence of the Lord as a member of the company of Christians.

The meaning of fellowship was made vivid for me several years ago in Europe while my wife and I were touring with six college students. On our way south through Yugoslavia to Greece, we decided rather impulsively to visit Bulgaria. It was not on our published itinerary, but when we discovered how close Sofia was to Belgrade, at the last moment we turned left and headed our Volkswagen microbus over the mountains toward that fabled city. Our border crossing was not pleasant. It was apparent that the Bulgarians were not exactly thrilled that we Americans had deigned to visit their Communist country. But we persisted and they reluctantly admitted us. We arrived in Sofia about nightfall and began our search for a campground. By the time we finally found one our enthusiasm had waned considerably. We drove in between a large illuminated sculptured red star, towering over the entrance on one side and a more-than-life-sized statue of a Bulgarian Communist leader (at least that was what we assumed) on the other side. As we pulled up to the guardhouse, the bar dropped behind our vehicle, preventing any quick escape, a thought that had crossed my mind. Our passports were demanded of us, something we had experienced in other campgrounds, but the routine seemed more ominous behind the Iron Curtain. We pitched our tents, tried to relax a little, and turned in. As I lay in my tent, hoping I'd be able to sleep and blaming myself for giving in to our group impulse, I heard Kathy leave the girls' tent and walk over to the boys'.

"John," she called out to her brother, "do you realize that nobody in America knows where we are?" Her nervousness did nothing to ease my own.

We were experiencing what it means to be out of fellowship. We were in a strange, alien country, surrounded by people speaking a language we could not understand, governed by a government hostile to our own. Although we were in Bulgaria, we were not of it: we had practically nothing in common with our host country. We were surrounded by Bulgarians, but we were alone. Our consolation was in one another; we shared the same plight, communicated in the same language, and depended on one another for solace and safety. We may have temporarily severed our connection with America, but we had one another.

We were better off than many isolated souls whose world is equally hostile and strange, but who belong to no group in which they can find comfort. It is not surprising that the earliest Christians turned so readily to one another. When they embraced Christ they were rejecting the alien gods of their Gentile culture or the legalistic strictures of their Jewish heritage. They could no longer feel at home with non-Christians. They who had formerly been alienated from God (Ephesians 2) now found themselves at home with Him but strangers and sojourners in their own land. They had to have one another, because their former companions really "had no idea where" they were. They *had* to devote themselves to fellowship in the shared Christian life.

Unfortunately, the early devotion to one another was gradually lost in the church's subsequent centuries. A brief look at church architecture gives evidence of how far the church has departed from those simpler, closer days. The new Christians met in one another's homes at first. There were no church buildings and they undoubtedly were not even wanted. What the believers needed was the frequent reassurance that comes from being together with people of like faith and values. In fact the purpose for preaching, John says (1 John 1:3), is "that you may have *fellowship* with us . . . and our *fellowship* is with the Father and with his Son Jesus Christ." Those first-century Christians treasured their shared life. To visit the towering cathedrals of Europe, however, is to realize that when the church became married to the state, Christian fellowship gave way to the pompous splendor of organized religion. The informal gatherings in the humble warmth of Christian homes were forgotten in the formal grandeur of medieval worship; the simple Communion metamorphosed into the elaborate mass and baptism was no longer the dedicatory act of a penitent believer but the initiation rite of an unknowing infant being born into the church as he was born into the state.

I admire the beauty of the great cathedrals, but prefer the humble little church building I knew in my childhood and youth. It did not have the long narrow nave of the Gothic style; instead, it was a square room with curved pews. It was possible from almost any seat in the room to see every other one. I remember our Sunday morning ritual—one not printed in the bulletin but observed by almost all the worshipers. Immediately after being seated we would look around the room at every pew, to check up on our fellow members, to see who was there and who was missing (and who was wearing what and sitting with whom). To watch this ritual you would soon conclude that we were there not only to worship the Lord but also to check up on fellow Christians. Exactly! That is the nature of the church's fellowship: We worship the Lord and check up on one another. Both acts are important.

Actually, we do more than that. We treat our fellow members like players on a championship baseball team. Back in 1976 the Cincinnati Reds were at the height of their power. They took the World Series over the Yankees in four games that year. They played superb ball. Joe Morgan, their dynamic second baseman, explained their winning strategy in a locker room interview:

> I think ours is a super club. The key is that we pick each other up. We made mistakes and then other guys covered up for them. I made an error and we got bailed out of it by some good play. That's how we won all year, one guy picking up the other.

That's fellowship. We share our lives not only with the Lord, but with one another in the church. We check up on one another and then, when we see one stumble or hurt himself, we pick him up. We Christians have assumed, if you please, unlimited liability for each other. Unlike an insurance policy, which limits the company's responsibility in case of a policyholder's disability, the Christian church shares fully in the needs of the members. The Macedonian Christians, for example, who were afflicted with poverty themselves, nonetheless begged earnestly to assist the Christians in Jerusalem. They pleaded with Paul "for the favor of taking part in the relief of the saints . . ." (2 Corinthians 8:4). This sentence literally means that they "requested the grace and *fellowship*" of relieving their fellow Christians. They cared and wanted to share. We may call it contribution or offering or participation—it means sharing. Fellowship strikes the pocketbook, demands monetary sacrifice. If you are genuinely in fellowship with another, you care enough to share even the little that you have. This is underscored in 2 Corinthians 9:13:

> Under the test of this service, you will glorify God by your obedience in acknowledging the gospel of Christ, and by the generosity of your *contribution* for them and for all others.

That word *contribution* is *koinonia*, fellowship. In Romans 15:26 we encounter the same meaning:

> For Macedonia and Achaia have been pleased to make some *contribution* for the poor among the saints at Jerusalem.

They are entering into fellowship with the Jerusalem Christians; the concrete expression of their fellowship is the monetary contribution.

That Christian fellowship means financial sharing is a difficult lesson for American Christians to learn. We have been nurtured on selfishness; generosity is a violation of our "Me First" creed. Private property is the supreme good, we have been taught. We measure the stature of a person by the amount of money and private property he has accumulated. What a distance we have come from the earliest Christians, many of whom believed that even owning private property was against God's will. The fourth century leader Chrysostom, for instance, called such ownership theft. "God has invested capital with you," he said. "It is not your property, but a loan by him, made to give you opportunity to exercise mercy on those who are in need." What you have is God's, and He wants it used to bring mercy to the needy. One of our contemporary Christians seconds Chrysostom's teachings, adding, "Any surplus means, any idle capital that is not used to relieve the burden of the needy, is similar to stolen goods." That statement may be debated, but what cannot be debated is the eagerness with which the earliest Christians grasped the meaning that the fellowship of the church involves the sharing of one's total life, including possessions.

Acts 2:44, 45 states that "all who believed were together and *had all things in common; and they sold their possessions and goods and distributed them to all, as any had need.*" Acts 4 repeats the theme: "The company of those who believed were of one heart and soul, and no one said that any of the things which he possessed was his own, but they had everything *in common*" (4:32). That is fellowship. The believers held that everything in their lives was now to be controlled by the Spirit of Christ. Initially, therefore, they adopted a form of godly communism, pooling their financial resources, claiming private ownership of nothing. The impracticality of the arrangement soon became evident, however, and the broader principle of fellowship was applied as the final solution, with love-motivated sharing characterizing those Christians who had been caught up by Christ's exemplary love.

Thus for Paul, the collection he gathered from the Gentile churches on behalf of the poor in Jerusalem was not to be interpreted as a gesture of liberality; it was instead an expression of fellowship in Christ, of the shared life of all believers. No Christian could be insensitive to a brother's pain. The collection would be proof to the Jewish Christians that the Gentile Christians were really their brothers and sisters in Christ; the money would signal their oneness in the Lord. The exalted word *koinonia* can be readily used to refer to the taking of an offering as well as a reference to their community of belief in Christ. *Koinonia* is a further reminder that nothing the Christian possesses is his own. He can be generous with everything that he calls his, because he acknowledges God's ownership of everything; he is but a steward or manager of what God has invested in him.

Until a believer has grasped the truth that "the earth is the Lord's and the fullness thereof" he finds it hard to be in community with other believers. He wants to hoard and protect what he mistakenly claims to be exclusively his. It hurts him to give up anything, but he especially resists giving up his money. Yet when James writes that "religion that is pure and undefiled before God and the Father is this: to visit orphans and widows in their affliction" (1:27), he isn't directing us to make a social call. He means, as Acts 6 makes so evident, that we must do all we can to relieve their distress. That's fellowship.

This application of *fellowship* was faced recently by a church that had contributed generously to the building of a retirement home for the congregation's aged. When it was discovered, however, that Christians could live in the home only so long as they could pay their own way, the church became alarmed. That meant a widow could use up all her life's savings and then be turned out of the home with nothing. The church met the challenge by developing a fund to guarantee that their aged could stay and receive care for as long as they lived, no matter how much it cost, and the church would assume the liability. Fellowship requires no less than this. You don't stop sharing when *they* run out of money.

Fellowship in the church, then, means full sharing of life and possessions. Since God owns everything, we claim exclusive rights to nothing. What is ours is His and what is His is ours to use for His purposes. The Christian church today is still devoted to fellowship. Because we care, we share.

For Further Consideration

1. What are some English translations of the Greek word *koinonia?* What do all these words have in common?
2. How does the Communion service dramatize the church's fellowship?
3. Why was the church's fellowship so important to the early Christians? Do today's Christians have the same need?
4. What does a church's architectural design tell about the nature of the congregation that meets in it?
5. This chapter says that the nature of the church's fellowship involves

checking up on and picking up one another. Do you agree? How does your church perform these ministries?

6. Do you think that this statement might be a little extreme? "We have assumed unlimited liability for one another." How would you word the statement?

7. How important is the giving of our money as an act of worship and fellowship?

8. How should modern Christians react to the statement in Acts 2 that "all who believed were together and had all things in common; and they sold their possessions and goods and distributed them to all, as any had need"?

CHAPTER TEN

The Church That Cares

(Matthew 25:31-46)

The Christian community is a great family of sharing, as we discovered in the last chapter. Its overflowing love does not stop there, however. Not only do church members live with a constant eye on the needs of their fellow members; they are equally concerned to serve the whole human community within which their church lives. They have come to realize that their salvation in Christ is not an isolated, vertical relationship between themselves and God, but a triangular, embracing fellowship including God, self, and others. It is true that on the Day of Pentecost, when the conscience-stricken audience of Peter asked, "Brethren, what must we do?" they were told to yield themselves to Christ in repentance and baptism. Those were individual acts. But it is also true that they were added to one another immediately, and subsequent development of the early church was one of reaching out to those beyond their ranks. "I have no silver and gold, but I give you what I have " (Acts 3:6).

When Jesus was asked to summarize the Old Testament into the greatest commandment of all, He did so with a commandment in two parts: "You shall love the Lord your God with all your heart, and with all your soul, and with all your mind. . . . You shall love your neighbor as yourself" (Matthew 22:37-39). Love for God could not be divorced from love of neighbor. Salvation has social implications.

Jesus made this general principle come to life on two occasions. In the first one, a lawyer stood up to put Him to the test by asking, "Teacher, what shall I do to inherit eternal life?" This time the lawyer gave the great twofold commandment. When Jesus assured him this was the correct answer and that obedience to it would lead to life, the lawyer asked his famous loophole-seeking question, "But who is my neighbor?" Then Jesus told His peerless parable of the good Samaritan, forcing His interrogator to admit that the man who showed mercy on the robbery victim was the neighbor.

We are all familiar with this parable. What is often overlooked, however, is that Jesus tells it in response to the initial question of eternal salvation. To be saved one must love not only God but one's neighbor.

That this is not an isolated teaching of Jesus is proved by Mark 10:17ff. This is the famous incident in which the rich young man kneels before Jesus and asks the same question that the lawyer put to him, "Good Teacher, what must I do to inherit eternal life?" In this case, Jesus reviews several of the Ten Commandments with him and, discovering the young man observant of these points of law, adds, "You lack one thing; go, sell what you have, and give to the poor, and you will have treasure in heaven; and come, follow me." Nowhere else does Jesus make the selling of one's possessions a prerequisite to salvation. In this case He must have discerned that the man's dependence upon his material wealth was coming between him and God; a dependence perhaps expressed in failure to share with the poor. We must conclude that for the rich young man, to be saved one must love not only God but one's neighbor.

In both cases the men were laboring under a common religious misconception of God. They believed that God cares primarily about himself; thus so long as they praised Him and observed the sacrifices and rituals of religion, their destiny was secure. (Although we might ask why they bothered to raise the issue with Christ—could they have had some doubts about their security?) They failed to perceive that Jesus stood firmly on the tradition of the Old Testament prophets, whose message was uttered so forcefully by Amos:

I hate, I despise your feasts,
   and I take no delight in your solemn assemblies.

Even though you offer me your burnt offerings and cereal offerings,
   I will not accept them,
and the peace offerings of your fatted beasts
   I will not look upon.
Take away from me the noise of your songs;
   to the melody of your harps I will not listen.
But let justice roll down like waters,
   and righteousness like an everflowing stream.

(Amos 5:21-24)

God can do quite well without our offerings; the poor cannot.

Matthew 25 records Jesus' vision of the end times. Here, too, he rather surprisingly links social concern with personal salvation. "When the Son of man comes in his glory," He tells His followers, all the nations of the earth will be gathered before Him for judgment. The criterion He will use on that occasion will not be doctrinal purity or conscientious observance of religious feasts and rituals, but unselfish social concern:

> Then the King will say to those at his right hand, 'Come, O blessed of my Father, inherit the kingdom prepared for you from the foundation of the world; for I was hungry and you gave me food, I was thirsty and you gave me drink, I was a stranger and you welcomed me, I was naked and you clothed me, I was sick and you visited me, I was in prison and you came to me' (Matthew 25:34-36).

Several will be surprised, not knowing that in offering some help "to one of the least of these" they were actually performing religious service, that is, assisting Christ.

In the Sermon on the Mount Jesus utters the same theme: "Not every one who says to me, 'Lord, Lord,' shall enter the kingdom of heaven, but he who does the will of my Father who is in heaven. On that day many will say to me, 'Lord, Lord, did we not prophesy in your name, and cast out demons in your name, and do many mighty works in your name?' And then will I declare to them, 'I never knew you; depart from me, you evildoers' (Matthew 7:21-23).

What is the standard of salvation? Obviously religiosity is not enough. It is too easy to manipulate the practices of piety for self gain, like one businessman in a Berry's World cartoon who says to another, "C'mon, Harry, give it to me straight. Is there good money in being 'born again'?" When religion becomes the vogue it is easy to jump on the religious bandwagon, shout one's alleluiahs and pray one's prayers, asking only the selfish question, "What must I do to be saved (for *me, myself*)?" Jesus' teachings will not allow us to so pervert the Christian faith, however.

Such a perversion was spectacularly popular earlier in this century. Dr. Russell H. Conwell, pastor of Temple Baptist Church in Philadelphia and founder of Temple University, before his death in 1925 had for 40 years preached his famous "Acres of Diamonds" sermons 6,000 times from coast to coast. It is not hard to explain its popularity: "Get rich, young man, for money is power," Conwell proclaimed. "I say you have no right to be poor. . . . Love is the grandest thing on God's earth, but fortunate is the lover who has plenty of money. . . ." This, the most popular sermon ever preached in America, sounds not at all like Jesus' instructions to the young man who had plenty of money.

Roman Catholic Bishop Topel of Spokane made the pages of TIME magazine in 1978 by his attempt to take Jesus seriously. He had been Bishop of Spokane for 22 years, but TIME reported that the bishop lived like a pauper. In 1968, after Vatican II emphasized the need for the Catholic Church to bear witness to poverty, Topel became convinced that God wanted him in a smaller house, to live like the poor. So he sold his bishop's mansion and bought a four-room frame house for $4,000. He spent no money for food, lived on what he could grow and what handouts he received. He kept the temperature in his house at 40 degrees, wore patched clothes and hand-me-down shoes from a dead priest (two sizes two big). At 75 he was still working, living on his social security, giving everything else away—and receiving much criticism. His defense? He wanted to obey Jesus.

That is one man's answer to the rather difficult question, "What must I do?" The concern of this chapter, however, is for the church. How does the church respond to Christ's teaching concerning social responsibility? Clearly, the church is the agency Christ established to continue His ministry to the hungry, thirsty, estranged, naked, sick, and imprisoned persons of this world. The church is Christ's provision for the needy. It is given to the world as a lifesaving station. But, as Halford Luccock has asked, "What would you think of the crew of a lifesaving station who gave all their attention to the station itself, made the quarters attractive, planted gardens, designed uniforms, provided music, and thus pleasantly occupied, shut out the roar of pounding breakers, driving ships and men to destruction on the rocks?" His disturbing question drives home the warning that many churches are precisely so occupied, having forgotten their call to be lifesavers. As a further thrust he adds, "How many churches, just at the time when the needs around them were growing greater, have packed up and followed 'the righteous' out to a new location in a pleasant residential section, where peace, perfect peace, reigns! In some such fashion we can get away from the disturbing cries and burdens of sin and need."

Unfortunately, the move away from sin also moves us far away from the One who came not to call the righteous, but sinners (Mark 2:17).

We have earlier established the fact that the Bible speaks of God's chosen people: In the Old Testament, the nation of Israel; in the New Testament, the church. But nowhere are God's chosen people allowed to think of themselves as being chosen for their own sake; they were chosen for the sake of the unchosen. By Abraham's seed *all* the nations of the earth would be blessed. Through the suffering of Mary, chosen to bring Jesus to birth, all are blessed. Through the suffering of Christ the world can be redeemed from slavery to sin and suffering; through the suffering of the church, the rescue mission continues, and only through its willingness to leave the comforts of the lifesaving station to go on dangerous assignments can the church be called the church.

That churches have a responsibility to care for their own was the subject of our last chapter. The fact that churches generally obey this injunction quite well leads to a disturbing problem, however. The churches of the poor will become, in time, comfortable middle-class congregations. This consistent pattern can be traced through the history of Christianity. H. Richard Niebuhr has demonstrated that the development of denominations is at first "the story of the religiously neglected poor, who fashion a new type of Christianity which corresponds to their distinctive needs." They then prosper because of their religious discipline, become more respectable, and then in turn neglect the poor they have left behind.

Niebuhr is right but disturbing. Since Jesus has sent us to the poor, how can we protect ourselves from slipping into comfortable conformity, worshiping with only our own kind, insulating ourselves from the discomforting demands of those beneath us on the social scale? The fact is, the church needs the poor as much as the poor need the church; without them the church is in danger of losing her Christly identity. Respectability and affluence can never be equated with Christlikeness.

The pattern Niebuhr points out has recurred so predictably in history that it gives credence to the diabolical interpretation of religion by men like Napoleon. Napoleon claimed to believe in an intelligence governing the physical world, but was far from an orthodox believer. Admitting that everything points to the existence of a God, he nevertheless fell far short of claiming belief in one, saying on one occasion that if he had to have a religion, he would worship the sun as the true god of the earth. Religion was invented by men, he said, to comfort the poor and keep them from killing the rich.

> I do not see in religion the mystery of the Incarnation but the mystery of the social order. Society cannot exist without inequality of property, an inequality which cannot be maintained without religion. It must be possible to tell the poor; 'It is God's will. There must be rich and poor in this world, but hereafter, and for eternity, there will be a different distribution.' Religion introduces into the thought of heaven an idea of equalization which saves the rich from being massacred by the poor.

One can hardly imagine a statement farther from the spirit of the Scriptures than this one. Yet when one surveys the history of Christianity, he finds that in century after century in country after country the church has aligned itself with the rich, the powerful, and the overbearing. Clergy have lived and ruled like princes, with little regard for struggling serfs. Giant cathedrals have risen from barren ground in which peasants huddle in mud huts. The spirit of Napoleon has repeatedly threatened to conquer the Spirit of Christ.

Where Christ's Spirit is, there is concern for the poor, a concern that makes itself known in diverse ways. It is not only concerned about the poverty of the poor, but works to rescue them from the clutches of loan sharks, the ravages of alcohol, the dehumanization of unemployment, the inhumanity of racism, the loneliness of age. No longer able to look on them as anyone other than precious persons for whom Christ died, the church on Christ's behalf offers forgiveness for sin, restoration for failure, generosity in place of the greed. The church recognizes that men have needs that no governmental agency, political party, labor union, social club, or benevolent institution can ever meet. The church, like Christ, is on the side of this world's underdogs.

Furthermore, the church recognizes that it is inadequate only to rescue the individual without correcting the system that has destroyed him. While the good Samaritan was right to help the wounded robbery victim on Jericho's road, surely something must be done to rid the road of the robbers. Is it enough to rescue the individual alcoholic without doing anything to loosen the alcohol industry's stranglehold on society? Can we be content with visiting the prisoner and overlooking the horrible inequities and forced squalor of our penal system? The church has a mammoth responsibility.

It is a responsibility from which we cannot turn, if we would be Christ's disciples. The cross compels us to take God's attitude toward human suffering. As He was unable to remain aloof but instead participated as a fellow sufferer, so He calls us to pick up a cross also. The disciple is not above the teacher.

Therefore Christians take care of their houses and lands, but houses and lands are not their first concern. They use their wealth to give aid to those who have less.

Therefore churches cannot become entertainment centers for the distraction and inspiration of members only.

Therefore churches must think long and hard thoughts before abandoning downtown areas for greener pastures in the suburbs.

Therefore churches dare not become mutual admiration societies, filled with the best people, "our" kind of people.

Therefore churches must never allow the needs of their building to dictate the nature of their programs. They must never build buildings while ignoring social needs.

Therefore the church must be the body of Christ, a body reaching out to the blind, the maimed, the poor, the outcast, the leper, the prostitute, the tax collector, the nobody.

Therefore let the church remember that the God who holds in His hand the fate of all humanity does not call His people to dwell in splendid comfort and worship in majestic cathedrals, but calls them to visit prisons and sickbeds and hovels, to bring good news to the neglected and ostracized, to walk beside the stragglers that society has left behind.

This is not a popular message today. But then, carrying the cross of Christ has never been popular.

For Further Consideration

1. Why did Jesus so often relate a question of eternal life to one's caring for his neighbor or giving to the poor?
2. What do the parable of the Good Samaritan and Jesus' instruction to the rich young man tell us about God?
3. Why does Jesus say in Matthew 25 that at the last judgment there will be many surprised persons?
4. Do you agree with this statement, "The church is Christ's provision for the needy"?
5. If God's chosen people "were chosen for the sake of the unchosen," what obligation does the Christian church have toward those outside her gates?
6. Does the church need the poor as much as the poor need the church?
7. Is there any truth in Napoleon's claim that religion was invented by men "to comfort the poor and keep them from killing the rich"?
8. What then shall we do about the poor and overlooked and the system that has so badly hurt them?

CHAPTER ELEVEN

The Church At Your House

(Hebrews 3:1-6; 1 Peter 2:4, 5)

We are so conditioned to equate *church* with *the building on the corner* that we read about the New Testament church without seeing one of the most obvious facts about it. In the beginning, the church met in houses, not in spacious worship buildings. In fact, the people of the church are described as a house:

> Now Moses was faithful in all *God's house* as a servant, to testify to the things that were to be spoken later, but Christ was faithful over *God's house* as a son. And *we are his house* if we hold fast our confidence and pride in our hope (Hebrews 3:5, 6).

> Come to him, to that living stone, rejected by men but in God's sight chosen and precious, and like living stones be yourselves built into a *spiritual house* . . . (1 Peter 2:4, 5).

> So then you are no longer strangers and sojourners, but you are fellow citizens with the saints and members of the *household of God,* built upon the foundation of the apostles and prophets . . . (Ephesians 2:19, 20).

The church is the house of God, like the nation of Israel before it. Moses labored in God's house as a servant, Hebrews says; his ministry ended when Christ was established over the house as God's Son. We who believe in Christ have now become the household of God, held together in His love as a family.

To the first Christians, these words were welcome indeed. Although many came to Christ as families, for others the decision was painful and the consequences worse. They were rejected by their own, ostracized by society, fired from their jobs, cut off from their former friends. They had become followers of the hated Nazarene. What they needed, more than anything else, was a new household. They found their new family in the church.

Since there was no church building, the early congregations met in members' houses. Several examples in Acts demonstrate the Christians' generous dedication of their houses to the Lord's work. After Paul was dramatically converted on the road to Damascus, he was welcomed into the house of Judas in Damascus. Peter stayed in the house of Simon the tanner in Joppa and found refuge in Mary's home, and Paul and Silas went from jail to the house of Lydia.

Homes were opened for the study of God's Word. Paul reports that he did not shrink from declaring to the Christians anything that was profitable, teaching them in public and from house to house (Acts 20:20). Sometimes the householders got into trouble. In Thessalonica the rabble attacked Jason's house, and others who harbored Christians in their homes fell under scrutiny by society in general. The house continued to play a vital role. Even when he was held under arrest in Rome, Paul invited his acquaintances into his home in order to teach them about the kingdom of God.

The affluence of later centuries, which enabled Christians to build central meeting halls—and later stately cathedrals—altered the nature of the church. Church became identified with buildings instead of people. In the beginning, church property was wherever the members lived; in subsequent centuries (including our own) church property was defined as the building and grounds owned by the church as a whole. The earliest Christians set a precedent that modern churches would be wise to follow. They considered it an honor to be able to invite their fellow believers into their homes.

By our standards, their houses were quite humble. Little rectangular things made of poor clay or mud, with a window perhaps, they consisted of one or maybe two rooms for the family, with another room for the animals. Some of the better houses had a guest room on the second story. That was all. Yet those Christians gladly shared what they had.

Increased affluence has introduced a disturbing paradox. With the advent of air conditioning and expanded square footage in our homes, we now have more space and comfort to share than ever before—but we share it less. We seal out neighbors as we seal out the heat or cold. We feel less desire for conversation, for our entertainment needs are met by the ever present television set. We live better than anyone else in the world, but we keep it all to ourselves. Even conscientious Christians have difficulty admitting that "the earth is the Lord's and the fullness thereof"—and that fullness includes our houses. Our dwellings are God's, a gift from Him to be used as a part of His house. When I shut the world out of my house I shut out His will.

So the modern Christian must ask himself: *Am I letting God use my house for His purposes?* If Pentecost were to be repeated in our town today, would we be able to accommodate 3,000 new members? Would we automatically think of opening up our homes for God's use? Would we imitate Priscilla and Aquila, those generous Christians who seemed always to have a church in their house (Romans 16:3, 5)?

Many New Testament churches today are enjoying fantastic growth because they have rediscovered the importance of "house churches." At least once a week Christians assemble in members' homes for "the apostle's teaching and fellowship, the breaking of bread and the prayers." They serve not only to strengthen the ties of Christian friendship, but are effectively winning nonmembers to the Lord, many of whom would never have consented to visit a large worship service on Sunday morning. One family recently spent several thousand dollars adding on to their house so they would have more room to accommodate the college young people that meet there every Wednesday night. Another family has just held a special dedication service in their newly purchased house, so that God and their Christian family would know that it is God's house; they want to use it for Him.

Tim LaHaye tells in one of his books of three couples who dedicated themselves to having dinner once a month in one of their homes with three other couples. After two years of their meeting together (and always including two other couples who were not members of the church), they had more friends and knew more people than anyone else in the church. They had also won many to Christ while at the same time growing spiritually to the point that one of the couples became missionaries to Ecuador, another couple became staff members of Campus Crusade, and the third couple became pillars in their local church. They had turned their houses into part of God's house.

In another church a Christian businessman regularly hosts parties for his business associates. He always includes some key people from his church so that they can mingle with his associates and quietly influence them for Christ. He has won several new members for his church in this subtle way.

The importance of homes in the growth of the kingdom cannot be overstated. The Methodist Church began in the eighteenth century in the homes of members—as did practically every other Christian movement throughout history, often because established denominations were hostile to renewal efforts. In the intimacy of small group meetings, Christians were able to express their love and care for one another in God's name; there they experienced genuine *koinonia*, sharing.

God's House Depends on Our Houses

Perhaps the necessity of our using our homes for Christ can best be illustrated by this unfortunately true story. A minister who was doing some remodeling on his house hired a young contractor to do the job. As the work progressed the two of them talked fairly frequently, and the minister invited him to church. He came and in fact joined the church. After a while, however, he quit attending. It was only several months later that the minister learned the reason. When he had come out of the navy, the young man said, he was drinking so hard that it was breaking up his family and hurting his business. When the minister talked to him about the church, he thought that it could be what he needed. But it didn't do him a bit of good. He told the minister that he would have been surprised to know what condition he had been in just a few hours earlier. Anyway, he stopped going to church, but shortly afterwards he got into Alcoholics Anonymous. He said that the first night he went a fellow came up to him and asked where he was eating lunch tomorrow and suggested they get together. One of the women came up and said, "Why don't you and your wife have dinner with us one night this week?" He said they really got a hold of him and as a result he hadn't had a drink in months.

In this case, Alcoholics Anonymous succeeded where the church had failed—by using principles that came initially from the church! AA members don't own a building—they have to use their homes to do the work of AA. Churches own buildings—but they still have to use their homes if they are really going to do the work of the church.

Any church today that desires renewal and growth must return to the New Testament precedent, which means returning to houses. Homes can do what formal church edifices cannot do. They can reach men and women who would never enter the sanctuary of the church. People will come to your house

—to study the Bible and learn about God. Having perhaps had negative experiences in Sunday school or worship, they want nothing to do with *church*—but they remain curious to know more of God and His Word. They will study in the nonthreatening environment of your home.

—to find answers to their problems. Unwilling to admit that their problems are spiritual, yet suspecting they might be so, your friends will welcome an opportunity to discuss them in an atmosphere of trust and acceptance. In church they expect criticism; in your home they anticipate sympathy.

—to make new friends. Most people are lonely, and the largeness of many churches increases their loneliness. To be able to meet new friends in your home is an attraction.

—to try something new. This restless generation is always on the lookout for new adventures. You can offer something they haven't tried before.

—to experience "church" without having to attend. In spite of all that is said against the church today, it still stands for a commendable morality and high ideals. People are not turned off by God, or even the church as an ideal, but by institutionalized religion. You can help them experience the real thing.

Good things happen in house churches. There a real faith-trust relationship can be built among individuals who may never before have known what it means really to belong. There they can learn what sharing means and experience the love of God as it is expressed by one member for another. There they see examples of Christian maturity—and the patience mature Christians demonstrate for the more immature ones. They gain new insights into Scripture as each participant in the discussion gives his particular understanding of the passage being studied. They learn to pray, at first hesitantly, then with greater confidence. And there, with the encouragement of other members, they learn to become Christian leaders themselves.

This chapter might seem to be promoting the wholesale return to house churches and elimination of church buildings. Nothing could be further from my intention. My argument is not "either church building or house church" but "both church building and house churches." For obvious reasons Christians began constructing large meeting halls just as soon as they could collectively afford to do so. They needed them! We still do. For large experiences in worship, for community services, for more effective teaching experiences, and for a host of other reasons church buildings can be effective tools for serving Christ. Nothing can quite equal the thrill of being present in a congregation when hundreds or even thousands of Christians are singing and praising God together.

Furthermore, our culture expects the use of buildings. Americans seem to demand that churches have an identifiable location, on property primarily dedicated to the worship of God. Missionaries in other countries have found the same need. In India, for example, with its historical tie to Hinduism, Indians who are accustomed to worshiping in shrines cannot imagine worship apart from a "holy place." Evangelism among the Hindus, then, is greatly facilitated by the use of church buildings.

So it would be folly to suggest that modern churches sell their buildings and make exclusive use of member's homes. It is equally foolish, however, to rely exclusively on the church's building and ignore the powerful impact of Christian homes upon the church and the community. We shall continue to use the structure on the corner of Tenth and Maple for the many needs only it can satisfy, but we shall also look upon the houses of the members as church property dedicated to God and available to be used to win the many who cannot be touched by anything offered within the church building. When church and home are working cooperatively for the extension of the kingdom of God, nothing can stop its growth.

For Further Consideration

1. What activities in your church could—and should—be moved out of the church building and into homes of the members?
2. In what way are you using your house for God's work?
3. Obviously our modern church buildings are an asset. List the ways in which they assist the work of the church.
4. What is not so obvious is that sometimes the buildings can be a liability. Can you think of some ways in which they hinder the work of the church?
5. How do our buildings influence the kind of program a church has?
6. Several examples are given in this chapter of ways Christians are using their houses for evangelism. Can you add others?
7. The emphasis in this chapter has been on new Christians. In what ways can older Christians benefit from "house church" experience?
8. An example is given from Alcoholics Anonymous. The power of AA is in members having the same problem helping each other. What other types of problems could be helped within the church if groups were established to meet their needs?

CHAPTER TWELVE

The Church
That Sends

(Matthew 28:19, 20; John 20:19-23;
John 17:20, 21)

The mission of the church begins with Jesus himself. "God had an only son," David Livingstone wrote, "and he was a missionary . . ." Jesus perceived himself in the same terms: "My food is to do the will of him who sent me, and to accomplish his work" (John 4:34).

His was not a self-appointed job; He was *commissioned (sent by)* God to accomplish a mission. Early in His ministry He returned to Nazareth, His home town, and in the synagogue He read the Scripture. Concluding the reading from Isaiah 61 He announced to His townspeople, "Today this Scripture has been fulfilled in your hearing." *God had sent Him* to preach good news to the poor, proclaim release to the captives and recovering of sight to the blind, set at liberty those who are oppressed, and proclaim the acceptable year of the Lord. He did not invent His calling: "The Spirit of the Lord . . . has anointed me." As one under orders, then, He visited the cities and villages of Palestine to complete the assignment of Isaiah 61. He was a missionary sent from God.

Jesus multiplied His effectiveness by transmitting God's commission to His disciples, making them missionaries also. "As the Father has sent me, even so I send you," He told them. Empowering them with the Holy Spirit, He sent them out to continue His mission.

> Go . . . and make disciples of all nations, baptizing them in the name of the Father and of the Son and of the Holy Spirit, teaching them to observe all that I have commanded you; and lo, I am with you always, to the close of the age (Matthew 28:19, 20).

Jesus had recruited them in order to train and send them. Further, His disciples were in turn to instruct the early Christians that they also were missionaries.

The book of Acts records the progress these missionaries made in building the church of Christ. While the book omits much that a general history would include, it fulfills its central purpose of recounting the success of these Spirit-led missionaries among Jews and Gentiles alike. Acts is about missions and missionaries, about Stephen who died preaching, about Philip who was elected a deacon but became an evangelist, about the cross-cultural missionary work of Peter and Paul and others, about the three thousand believers who soon became five thousand who grew to become many thousands more.

In the church's earliest days, every Christian felt compelled to share the gospel with another. It was not long, however, before the burning words of Jesus motivated the church to select certain especially qualified men to carry the gospel beyond the confines of Jerusalem. Jesus had promised His disciples,

> You shall receive power when the Holy Spirit has come upon you; and you shall be my witnesses in Jerusalem and in all Judea and Samaria and to the end of the earth (Acts 1:8).

As early as Acts 8 we read that the persecution that arose following Stephen's death scattered the Jerusalem Christians through the region of Judea and Samaria, and "those who were scattered went about preaching the word." Acts 11 reports that a missionary church had been established in the Gentile city of Antioch. Acts 13 and following chapters trace the church-planting mission of the apostle Paul and his companions. The church had already begun to obey Christ's commission.

Acts leaves no room for misunderstanding. Mission is the essence of the church. Emil Brunner has reminded us that mission is to the church what fire is to burning. The priority of the church's mission is to declare Jesus to the world in order to save men and women for today and forever. The church therefore preaches Christ and establishes churches that will in turn preach Christ and establish churches until all the world can be saved.

Motive

A missionary to the Orient explained his reason for going to the mission field. He said that several years earlier he had attended a solemn Communion service in America where there were more than 1,500 Christians in attendance. When the elements had been passed out, the presiding pastor asked, "Is there anyone who has been overlooked?" A missionary from India stood and said that 450 million in India had been omitted. There was a shocked silence, and then a missionary from the Philippines stood to announce that 30 million of his people had been omitted. One by one around the room these missionaries arose to speak in behalf of their people who had been omitted because they had no one to tell them of the love of Jesus.

What can be done for these overlooked ones? God still loves the world; He sent His son to save the world; His son commissioned His church to carry on His rescue mission. Therefore, Oswald Smith asks, "Why should so few hear the gospel again and again and again, when so many have never heard it once?" We are called to lost peoples; we are called to sacrifice ourselves on their behalf as Christ sacrificed himself on ours.

One of the great names in missions in the last century is Hudson Taylor, founder of the China Inland Mission. On a Sunday morning in 1865 he is reported to have rushed out of a crowded church in Brighton, England, gasping for air, because the atmosphere of smug piety had stifled him. In describing that experience, he said, "Unable to bear the sight of a congregation of a thousand or more Christian people rejoicing in their own security, while millions were perishing for lack of knowledge, I wandered out on the sands alone in great spiritual agony." He doubted the super-spirituality of a congregation that could smugly ignore his beloved Chinese people. He would undoubtedly have applied the words of Dr. Clarence P. Oberndorf, late professor of psychiatry at Columbia University, to churches. Dr. Oberndorf told a convention of psychologists that "mental health depends upon the extent of awareness that a person has attained in his relationship with his fellow beings." Taylor could have said that the mental health of a church depends upon the extent of that church's awareness of fellow Christians—or potentially fellow Christians—throughout the world.

Cost

Churches that take missions seriously, however, discover they cannot give lip service to Christ's cause. Christian missions have always been costly. Stephen was only the first of a list of Christian martyrs that is still growing. He died trying to spread the gospel. In the twentieth century, especially in Africa, hundreds of missionaries have died for their faith. A veteran Methodist missionary in Zaire had been told that he was on the hit list of the rebels. He said, in harmony with centuries of missionaries, "I have been on their hit list, that's right, but I don't worry about it because I am also on another list, God's. I say to God, You take over, I am yours." His was the spirit of David Brainerd, early American missionary to Indians, who said, "I cared not where or how I lived or what hardships I went through, so that I could win souls for Christ."

The cost is in dollars as well as dedicated lives. No church can boast that it takes Christ's mission seriously while giving the token ten percent to missions. American Christians are faced with a serious rethinking of their obligation in the rest of the world. We need no statistics to prove that America continues to earn the envy of a hungry world. We throw enough food into the garbage can daily to feed much of the starving population of the world. We build our magnificent churches and appoint them with all the comforts of home while our Christian brothers and sisters in developing countries struggle daily to find something to eat.

Yet even in America there are churches which are rising to the challenge of the world's needs. When members of the Eastminster Presbyterian Church in suburban Wichita, Kansas, learned that a disastrous earthquake struck Guatemala and destroyed thousands of homes and buildings, they immediately revised their new building program plans. They slashed the cost of their proposed building from $525,000 to $180,000, sent their pastor and two elders to Guatemala to see how they could help, then borrowed $120,000 from a local bank to rebuild 26 Guatemala churches and 28 Guatemalan pastors' houses.

The Wichita church was simply following the precedent of

New Testament Christianity. Paul's letter to Corinth includes his appeal for an offering from those Gentile Christians for their brethren, the Jewish Christians in Jerusalem. The principle to which he appeals is that of financial equality among Christians.

> I do not mean that others should be eased and you burdened, but that as a matter of equality your abundance at the present time should supply their want, so that their abundance may supply your want, that there may be equality. As it is written, 'He who gathered much had nothing over, and he who gathered little had no lack' (2 Corinthians 8:13-15).

Our obligation can be graphically illustrated. Let us reduce the world to 100 individuals living in one village. Of these, 67 would be poor; the rest would have from a sufficiency to an abundance. Only seven of the 100 would be North Americans, but these seven would spend one-half of the village money and eat one-seventh of all the food. They would have ten times as many doctors as all the rest. But what is worse, with succeeding years the seven would become richer while the other 93 would become poorer.

What further irritates is that some of the Americans try to evangelize the other 93, even as they throw away food the others desperately need. They build a bigger church while the 93 try to find adequate shelter for their families. The seven enlarge their bank accounts while most of the others have too little money to feed their families.

Now we begin to understand Paul's equality principle. We cannot hope to convince the poor either within or without the church that God really loves them so long as some of us parade in luxury while the rest fight with debilitating poverty. If we would imitate Jesus, who had no place to rest His head, we must be prepared readily to share what we have with the lost and needy not only in Jerusalem and Judea, but in Samaria and the rest of the world. Out of our abundance of wealth we must give money; out of our abundance of Christian leadership we must send missionaries.

Message

Romans 10 spells out the church's message:

> The word is near you, on your lips and in your heart (that is, the

word of faith which we preach); because, if you confess with your lips that Jesus is Lord and believe in your heart that God raised him from the dead, you will be saved (10:8, 9).

What a magnificent statement Paul makes. We are not saved by any works of our own, any ritual, regulation, or memorized formula. We are saved by faith in Jesus Christ—and so is everyone else.

In their haste to meet the crying social needs of the world, many churches have devoted enormous amounts of money and manpower to their missions. They have established hospitals and clinics where no medical assistance had existed before; they have founded schools and colleges to bring enlightenment to uncounted millions of former illiterates; they have taught new methods of agriculture, provided political and economic counsel, and attempted everything else in their power to raise the standard of living for developing countries. Sometimes in their eagerness to help, they have overlooked the message. They have given "a cup of cold water," but have not always announced in whose Name they were giving it.

What distinguishes Christian missions from international relief, however, is Christ. Romans 10:10 insists that it is faith in Jesus that saves. John 14 says the same thing: "I am the way, and the truth, and the life; no one comes to the Father, but by me." Basic to all Christian missions is the saving message that "God so loved the world that he gave his only Son."

Romans 10:13 promises that "every one who calls upon the name of the Lord will be saved." But listen to this:

> How are men to call upon him in whom they have not believed? And how are they to believe in him of whom they have never heard? And how are they to hear without a preacher? And how can men preach unless they are sent? (10:14, 15).

We might add for those of us who stay home, "How are they to be sent unless you and I give them the money to go?"

Thus all Christians are involved in the church's missionary work. We are either the missionary or the missionary's supporters. We participate in the work in the spirit of John Wesley, who correctly echoed Augustine's conviction that the servant of God ministers for the whole church in the whole world:

I must have a whole Christ for my salvation;
I must have a whole Bible for my staff;
I must have a whole church for my fellowship;
I must have the whole world for my parish.

We are all partners in taking the entire message of the gospel to all the hurting world.

Method

There is little debate among evangelical Christians that the church has a mission throughout the world. There is a real debate, however, about the methods we should use in sending the gospel. When we say "missions," what do we mean? What activities constitute the church's mission? As we have just seen, many good works go by this title: radio ministries, publishing and distributing Christian literature, benevolent and social activities like hospitals and clinics and physical rehabilitation for the handicapped, educational institutions like Bible institutes and liberal arts or vocational colleges. In some totalitarian countries, missionaries can even be found actively plotting political revolution; they call their work missions. In others, their primary concern is agricultural or industrial assistance.

While all these good works have value, the church needs to be reminded of Christ's very clear marching orders: "Go . . . and make disciples . . . baptizing them . . . teaching them to observe all that I have commanded you " (Matthew 28:19, 20). The book of Acts is evidence enough that the church obeyed the orders. To make disciples, to gather them in clusters of believers, to nurture them in Christ so that they in turn can make disciples—that was the early church's program. The apostle Paul is presented in Acts as the leading missionary. His activities were single-minded. Everywhere he went he challenged his hearers to accept Christ as their Lord; then he led those who responded to his appeal into fellowship with one another in a new community of believers, a church of Christ. To Paul, missions was church planting. That remains the primary method of effectively spreading the gospel today.

The challenge is as great as ever, however, as the following report in the July 1977 Association of Church Missions Committees *Newsletter* illustrates:

While tremendous progress has been made in missions in the last few decades, with 1,000 third world churches now being born each week, nevertheless intensive analysis reveals one central and disturbing fact—84% of the non-Christians of the world are beyond the reach of virtually all efforts of all mission agencies as well as beyond the normal evangelistic reach of presently established churches, even those "on the mission field." The great majority of present missionary work is not in evangelism at all. Moreover, most of the evangelism that is being done is directed toward the immediate neighbors of Christians or toward nominal Christians associated with the existing church.

A *World Vision* report in the same year (based on the eleventh edition of *Mission Handbook*) states that of the total Protestant mission force of 55,000 (of whom 37,000 come from the U.S. and Canada), 28% are primarily involved in establishing churches or carrying out direct evangelism, 25% are involved with supporting existing national churches, while the remaining 47% are involved in a wide variety of ministries like education, literature, broadcasting, medicine, etc. Much more emphasis must be given to the church's primary evangelistic task.

Missions and Social Action

Since the priority in Christian missions is evangelism and church planting, what is the church's responsibility to relieve human suffering through direct social action? The answer is as simple to state as it is difficult for the uninitiated to understand. Evangelism and church planting lead directly to the alleviation of poverty and injustice; sometimes, as in many sections of today's troubled world, the Christian message is a revolutionary one, with dedicated Christian leaders at the forefront of the struggle against tyranny and for human rights. The gospel proclaims that all men are equal and of eternal worth in God's eyes. Nothing more effectively destroys caste systems and cultural prejudices than the realization that those peoples whom one formerly despised are the very ones for whom Christ died. The new life in Christ is not just spiritual equality; it is replete with social, political, economic implications. When Christian missions make it their first priority to win men and women to Jesus Christ and welcome them into the embrace of the church, they are paving the way for social action on a grand scale.

The Scriptures will not allow Christians to turn a blind eye to the needs of those within the Christian family or without:

116

> If your enemy is hungry, feed him; if he is thirsty, give him drink (Romans 12:20).

> If any one has the world's goods and sees his brother in need, yet closes his heart against him, how does God's love abide in him? (1 John 3:17).

> When you give a feast, invite the poor, the maimed, the lame, the blind, and you will be blessed, because they cannot repay you (Luke 14:13, 14).

> If a brother or sister is ill-clad and in lack of daily food, and one of you says to them, "Go in peace, be warmed and filled," without giving them the things needed for the body, what does it profit? So faith by itself, if it has no works, is dead (James 2:15-17).

These verses only suggest the wealth of Scriptures instructing Christians to share their abundance with others in want. Taken seriously, the Scriptures are a handbook for economic redistribution for social inclusiveness, for political evolution and revolution.

Missions and the Local Church

When we speak of the church's mission, we mean the local church. In the New Testament, the apostles established local churches, introduced believers into the fellowship of local churches, ordained leaders for local churches, and wrote their letters to these churches. Great denominational hierarchies were unheard of; mission agencies were a much later development. Even today, with hundreds of agencies and parachurch organizations to assist the church to accomplish its mission, the money is still given and missionaries are still recruited in local churches.

What should the church do to fulfill Christ's commission? Many things:

1) It must preach the full Biblical message, including Christ's uncompleted commission to go into all the world.

2) It must make the apostles' priority the first concern of its program. God sent Christ and Christ sent the disciples; the church as Christ's body is charged with the same responsibility. So long as the world remains unevangelized, every local church is under orders. Let the budget reflect God's priorities.

3) It must pray for God to raise up workers for His worldwide vineyard. Its prayers cannot be general, "God help the

missionaries." Let the church offer up her finest young people—and older people—for mission service; let the church pray to be used sacrificially for the service.

As James Van Buren has succinctly stated,

> the local assembly is the place where the church *is* a worshiping, witnessing, and working unit. It is the place where missions can best be *taught*, where missionary enthusiasm can best be *caught*, and where missionary recruits can best be *sought*.

He recommends that missions be taught in education departments from the beginner and primary through the youth and adults, as well as in worship services.

4) It must insist that those missionaries supported by the church have an intelligent, Biblical strategy. Let the winning of persons to Christ be first. And let not that high-sounding phrase be a cover for "missions-in-general" instead of real church planting in particular.

5) It must not be so independent as a congregation that it refuses to cooperate with others in supporting mission teams that are fulfilling the Great Commission.

6) It must work at missions with the intensity of Oswald J. Smith. No modern preacher has done more for world evangelism than this Canadian minister. He always made it very clear that he was a missionary first, even before being a pastor or author or hymn-writer. He tried to go himself; in fact, he went, but ill health forced him home. So he did the only thing he could: he gave his abundant energy to finding and sending substitutes.

So must every local church. The whole world is still waiting for us to obey Christ's commission. Let us go or send; let us pray with all our hearts that this sin-sick world can be rescued; let us send our finest to the rescue.

For Further Consideration

1. In what way is it correct to call Jesus a "missionary"?
2. In what way is it correct to call Jesus' disciples missionaries?
3. What is the mission of the church?
4. How do you answer Oswald Smith's question, "Why should so few

hear the gospel again and again and again, when so many have never heard it once?"
5. What do missions cost?
6. How should we apply Paul's equality principle to the mission of the church?
7. What is the message of missions?
8. What is the best mission method?
9. What more can your church be doing to win the lost world to Christ?

CHAPTER THIRTEEN

Who Runs This Organization?

(Ephesians 4:11-16)

A discussion of church organization has been delayed until this late chapter, in order to give the subject the same secondary emphasis the New Testament gave it. In the apostolic church, first a group of believers in Christ was assembled and then an organization was developed to meet their needs and purposes. Matters of administration were not allowed to dominate the activities of the group; only minimal organization was adopted, just enough to get the job done.

New Testament churches seemed to function well with their simple procedures. Twenty centuries later, however, there is much confusion about the ideal structure that churches should adopt. Adolf Harnack, in his *Constitution and Law of the Early Church*, theorizes that there were two classes of officials in the apostolic church. One class was composed of men endowed by the Holy Spirit with certain charismatic qualities; they had authority over all congregations. The second class consisted principally of elders and deacons; they had only local authority.

Several other students of the early church believe there was no one form of church organization to be found in all the churches; instead, they argue that there were several types of organization, depending upon geographical areas and cultural differences. Congregational, presbyterian, and episcopal forms of church government have had their defenders, with each one claiming Biblical precedent for his position.

These disagreements arise from the fact that organizational matters were not the primary concern of Biblical writers; they left no detailed blueprint to be universally imitated by succeeding generations. However, to deny a blueprint is not to deny that the New Testament presents an ideal of church order, for one clearly emerges from Acts and the epistles.

That ideal originates in the church's strong sense of purpose in fulfilling Christ's commission to make disciples. In the act of making disciples and nurturing them, early church leaders encountered certain difficulties. There were problems in worship, teaching, disciplining, benevolence, and moral conduct in addition to the broader set of problems concerning the relations of congregations with each other and with society at large. Leadership problems arising with the missionary expansion of the church also arose. Following the inspired leadership of the apostles and prophets, the churches adopted such organization as necessary to resolve these difficulties. They worried very little about titles; the real concern was to select leaders of sterling quality who would work, not just hold office. By the end of the apostolic period two titles were generally used to indicate the division of manpower: elder or *presbyter* meant generally the same as bishop, *overseer*; and deacon, which is best translated *servant*.

In the beginning each congregation governed its own affairs, a fact that accounts for the diversity to be found from congregation to congregation. It is also apparent that congregational autonomy did not mean independence so much as interdependence. There was a strong sense that congregations of believers belonged to each other. In the New Testament there are examples of interchurch cooperation in three major areas: the establishing of new churches (the ministry of Paul), the settling of disputes that threatened to destroy the unity of the churches (the Jerusalem conference), and the pooling of financial resources to assist poverty-stricken fellow believers (the offering for Jersualem Christians). Congregations were not in competition with one another; the enemy was the world, not another church in the kingdom. They needed and supported one another in their crusade for Christ.

Modern churches that try to follow New Testament examples in the governing of congregations do not always find the going easy. Most of today's denominations and cults have resolved their difficulties with a strong centralized organization that dictates the policies to local congregations. "Who runs this organization?" is a question that Roman Catholics do not have to ask, for example, since lines of authority are spelled out in detail. Whether a denomination's hierarchy is organized in the presbyterian or episcopalian form, local churches generally follow the direction of their national or regional leaders.

But who runs the church that belongs to no denomination? To say that a local congregation is autonomous means that there is no authority outside the local body. But within that body, who is in charge? Are policies dictated by congregational vote, or by the elders, or by a board of elders and deacons, or by the pastor, or a ruling layman? What is the relationship of the constitution and by-laws to the New Testament? To what extent do the church's traditions dictate today's policies?

We should perhaps approach the topic indirectly, by discussing some current misconceptions which are popular among independent New Testament churches.

The church is a democracy. This is one of the most prevalent misconceptions among democratic American Christians. Brought up to revere the American political system, with its emphasis upon the right of every citizen to cast his vote, Americans like to organize their churches to imitate the nation's political structure, with two houses of Congress (elders and board), and a balance of power (executive/pastor, legislative/board, and judicial/elders), with the general populace (congregation) having final authority.

It is impossible to find that pattern in the New Testament. In the first place, when the apostolic churches were being formed, American democracy was nearly 1800 years away. The earliest Christians were Jews; the idea that fathers, mothers, and older children should all have equal vote in spiritual matters would have been inconceivable to them. Elders ruled their synagogues. The earliest churches therefore selected their oldest and wisest men to lead them, just as the oldest and wisest men of the Jewish community led the synagogues. Their decisions were not subject to review or rejection by the congregation at large.

We can see the folly of this supposition by some modern analogies. Would we want matters of our physical health to be

122

settled by majority vote, or do we seek to follow the advice of the wisest, most highly qualified physicians we can find? In legal matters, would we assemble our friends together and take a vote to decide what course we should take, or would we seek the counsel of the wisest, most highly qualified lawyer we could find? It seems rather strange that in matters of spiritual consequence we would elect men of spiritual maturity to lead the congregation, then subject their decisions to ratification by the lowest common denominator, the congregational vote. The church is not a democracy.

The church is a dictatorship. Realizing that a strictly democratic organization is without Biblical precedent, some Christian leaders have gone to the other extreme. They point to the apostle Paul who, in establishing churches, appointed elders and ruled with total authority, at least in the early stages of a church's life. They also note that the largest, most rapidly growing churches in the world today are run by pastors who are in total control of the church's operation. The pastor of the church thus uses his board of deacons or elders as his advisory committee only; they are without power to contradict his decisions. He is revered as God's man for that church.

That this is the most efficient organization there can be no question. That it can be justified from the New Testament is open to debate. The apostles were the unchallenged leaders of the apostolic church, that is true. But they acted in careful cooperation with one another, and they sought the counsel of the church at large (Acts 6; Acts 15). Undoubtedly strong personalities dominated, but these strong personalities so cared for the body as a whole that they refused the dictator role and worked in harmony with one another for the unity and the growth of the church. As students of political and church history agree, too much government leads to tyranny and too little government leads to anarchy. The apostles avoided both extremes. They were strong, Spirit-led leaders, but they refused to become tyrants. The church is not a dictatorship.

The modern church is a business. While most independent congregations adopt the political model for church government, in these same churches there are usually strong businessmen who cannot help reminding their fellow members, "The modern church has become a business, therefore it must be run like a business." It is a hard argument to refute when a church has a budget of half a million dollars, a dozen employees, extensive property holdings and a multifaceted program. There must be budgets and cost control and long-range planning. But if the church is not careful, the pastor becomes an administrative manager, the elders a board of directors, the members stockholders and the potential members customers. For this model there is no New Testament precedent, either.

It cannot be debated that some good business practices must be employed, but the church dare not become a business. Church members are pilgrims, walking by faith, following a Leader who has shown little patience with the paraphernalia of institutions. Congregations are held together by faith, hope and love, not budgets and pledges. They are called to mission and ministry, not profits and balance sheets. They can exist without buildings or employees, but not without caring and sharing. They encourage each member to offer his spiritual gifts to the Lord in service; they organize sufficiently to accomplish their God given tasks. They resist the temptation to manipulate members for the sake of the organization because they are here to serve, not to "make a profit." The church is not a business.

The modern church is like other human organizations. This is the crux of the problem. In reaching out for a comparison for the church, whether that be in government or business or social clubs, we have overlooked one striking fact: there is no parallel for the church. It is not a human organization; it is a divine/human organism. Its analogy cannot be found in any organization as organization. Paul, recognizing this fact, found his best comparison in the human *body*. Of that body Christ is the head, the Spirit is the infusing power, and we are the functioning members. We are thus in Christ, He is in us; we are inseparable from one another, indispensable to one another. No member has any more authority than any other, except as appointed for the purpose by the Head. Our purpose is to function; if He chooses to call one or another of us to be a leading servant, He may.

With this background, we are now ready to look at Ephesians 4:11-16, where Paul offers several important principles for church organization.

1. *God gave the church leaders.* "His gifts were that some should be apostles . . ." begins this section. Paul does not elaborate upon this principle; he assumes it. The church is the

124

body of Christ, indwelt by the Holy Spirit, directed by the Lord himself. Since He has been following His eternal purposes, "even as he chose us in him before the foundation of the world," all things about the church are under His control and subject to His direction. The leaders of the apostolic church were God-appointed men. He gave some men to the church as leaders, others as helpers. The point never to be forgotten is that God equips the church.

2. *God defined leadership as service.* He equipped the church with leaders who in turn equip the members to do the work of ministry. The leaders serve the servants. Jesus defines leadership in the same terms:

> You know that those who are supposed to rule over the Gentiles lord it over them, and their great men exercise authority over them. But it shall not be so among you; but whoever would be great among you must be your servant, and whoever would be first among you must be slave of all. For the Son of man also came not to be served but to serve, and to give his life as a ransom for many (Mark 10:42-45).

Following this principle, elders and deacons can never see themselves as "members of the Board of Directors" or title-holders on "the Official Board." They are the church's leading servants.

3. *God made method of appointment less important than character of appointees.* Ephesians mentions nothing of elections; the Bible does not spell out procedures by which congregations elect officers. These matters are left to the individual churches. There is no doubt, however, that only the most Christlike persons should be appointed, ones able to equip others and build up the church. The requirements are clearly spelled out in 1 Timothy 3 and Titus 1.

Sometimes church leaders were appointed by the evangelist (Acts 14:23); sometimes they were appointed by the overseers in cooperation with the congregation (Acts 6). It is obvious that there had to be consensus between leaders and followers. Once chosen, the leaders were given wide latitude in their decision-making.

4. *He charged the leaders to protect the unity of the body.* The Bible is nothing if not a realistic book. Even a quick reading of the New Testament epistles reveals that the church has always

125

consisted of persons of all types and temperaments for whom unity is no mean achievement. Christians must be "eager to maintain the unity of the Spirit in the bond of peace," Paul writes (Ephesians 4:3). Leaders are to care for the church "until we all attain to the unity of the faith and of the knowledge of the Son of God." (vs. 13) This is in accord with the theme of Ephesians: "to unite all things in him, things in heaven and things on earth" (1:10).

Jesus prayed for His disciples,

> I do not pray for these only, but also for those who believe in me through their word, *that they may all be one;* even as thou, Father, art in me, and I in thee, that they also may be in us, so that the world may believe that thou hast sent me (John 17:20, 21).

The oneness of the believers in Christ was expressed early in the church's life:

> Now the company of those who believed *were of one heart and soul,* and no one said that any of the things which he possessed was his own, but *they had everything in common* (Acts 4:32).

Without strong, loving leaders, such unity is impossible.

5. *He charged them to assist the growth of the body.* They were to help individual Christians grow spiritually and the entire body grow numerically. With a world full of lost and dying people, church overseers lead their maturing members in an attack upon the world's condition. They base their decisions on whether a proposed course of action will aid or impede the church's growth in spiritual and numerical ways. That is, they are men of vision. They willingly sacrifice their pleasures and comforts for the good of the church, but they exercise their judgment to the end that in every way the members may be edified and the church may become more like Christ.

The book of Acts emphasizes the growth of the church:

> 2:47 "And the Lord added to their number day by day . . ."

> 6:7 "And the word of God increased; and the number of the disciples multiplied greatly in Jerusalem . . ."

> 9:31 "So the church throughout all Judea and Galilee and Samaria had peace and was built up."

12:24 "But the word of God grew and multiplied."

16:5 "So the churches were strengthened in the faith, and they increased in numbers daily."

The Holy Spirit was leading the church, and the result He desired was growth. Today's leaders, inspired by the same Spirit, will lead their churches to the same result.

6. *He charged them to equip all members to serve.* Jesus prepared His disciples to serve; His disciples in turn prepared the early church to serve. Leaders of today's church are equippers also. Every wise pastor or teacher accepts the charge to educate and train less mature Christians to fulfill their ministry for Christ. The *saints* (Christians) are to minister; there are no exceptions. Paid preachers are not paid to serve on behalf of the membership at large; they are called to prepare the members to serve. All Christians are ministers, though not all ministers have the same task. Some preach, some evangelize, some take care of the members' physical needs, some do benevolent services, and so on (see Romans 12:3-8; 1 Corinthians 12:4-31). No Christian has been exempted from the service of the kingdom. Unfortunately, as Sam Shoemaker has written, "We have expected too little of our people and they have met our expectations."

It is only in serving the Lord that persons grow "to mature manhood, to the measure of the stature of the fulness of Christ." Church members are not only counted—they are measured. The standard is Christ: "until we all attain to . . . the measure of the stature of the fulness of Christ."

7. *He charged all members to grow to maturity.* Maturity means being able to assume responsibility for oneself and others. It is being able to stand firm in one's convictions without being tossed about by the latest fads and fashions of dress or doctrine. It implies a readiness to use God's gifts for God's purposes, thus doing one's part to build up the whole body in love.

Maturity means completion, even perfection. It is what Jesus had in mind when He told His disciples, "You, therefore, must be perfect, as your heavenly father is perfect" (Matthew 5:48). You must realize your God-given potential, fulfill your possibilities. You must not be satisfied with anything less than your best self and your church's realized potential. You must—in love—grow up.

For Further Consideration

1. How much organization should a church have? Is it possible to have too complex an organization?
2. What is the great danger faced by a democratically organized church? Is there any New Testament precedent?
3. What dangers are involved in a church that is totally run by one man?
4. To what extent should a church operate like a business? When is it too businesslike?
5. What other human organizations are like the church?
6. Where do church leaders come from?
7. How does the Bible define leadership?
8. Who is qualified to lead a church?
9. How important is church unity?
10. How does the church grow?

CHAPTER FOURTEEN

The Leaders
of the Church

(Ephesians 4)

A casual visitor to most modern churches would conclude that the function of the members is to help the minister run the program. He will hear the pastor plead for volunteers to teach Sunday-school classes, usher during worship services, and turn out in force for the annual spring cleaning day. His appeal seems to be, "Come and help me." As soon as a new member is added to the church's rolls, the minister is on the doorstep, ready to recruit him for service, often for a task that bears little relation to the religious impulse that brought the member into the church in the first place.

The New Testament ideal differs sharply from such practices. According to Ephesians 4, God gave the church leaders so that they could equip members ("saints") for the work of ministry. Leaders are to assist members to grow in Christ to full maturity, so that they will be able to stand firm in their convictions and assume adult responsibility in building up of the body of Christ.

Church leaders, then, are God's gifts to the church. In the beginning, His gifts included apostles and prophets, who so effectively led the church through the formative years that we still assert that the church was "built upon the foundation of the apostles and prophets, Christ Jesus himself being the cornerstone" (Ephesians 2:20).

Apostles

The term *apostle* appears 79 times in the New Testament, with slightly varying meanings. Jesus was an apostle of God (the word means "one who is sent"), as indicated by His use of the root word in apostle:

Mark 9:37 ". . . and whoever receives me, receives not me but him who sent me," *aposteilanta*.

John 20:21 "As the Father has sent me, even so I send you," *apestalken*.

Our term *missionary* is from the Latin word that is identical in meaning to the Greek *apostolein*, to send. The *sent one* is dependent on the *one who sends*, as Christ repeatedly asserted that He came to do the will of His Father and not His own. Furthermore, He was sent in order to send others.

In this respect Jesus differed from other religious leaders of His day. It was not uncommon for rabbis to have disciples who followed them, sitting at their feet to learn all they could from their master. They were disciples, learners. But Jesus transformed His disciples into apostles; from mere "learners" they became "ambassadors." Their discipleship period was training for their mission as His sent ones. He was preparing them for spiritual warfare, as a general instructs his troops. Then He sent them into battle.

Historically, the Christian church has reserved the term *apostle* for those who were personally prepared by Jesus. Most of the apostles were the original disciples whom Jesus selected to be with Him during His earthly ministry. Peter felt that in order to be an apostle one had to have been with Jesus from the time of His baptism by John and must have witnessed Jesus' resurrection. On these bases Matthias was chosen to replace the fallen Judas (Acts 1:21-26). The apostle Paul, who did not strictly meet Peter's criteria, nonetheless vigorously defended his right to be named among them because he had seen the risen Christ and been commissioned by Him to preach the gospel (1 Corinthians 9:1, 2; Acts 22:1-16). He considered that apostles were the chief of God's gifts to the church (1 Corinthians 12:28; Ephesians 4:11); their credentials were confirmed by miracles and signs (2 Corinthians 12:12). He insisted that the church defer to the leadership of the apostles ("Shall I come to you with a rod, or with love in a spirit of gentleness?" 1 Corinthians 4:21).

Prophets

Strictly speaking, a prophet is not so much a foreteller as a *forthteller*, although one who speaks for the truth of today's conditions and hints at the consequences of today's actions inevitably foretells the future as well. From the beginning, prophecy was characteristic of the early church. There was no written New Testament, of course, in the early days of Christianity. Divinely inspired speakers were trusted to speak a word from God to their contemporary problems. Further, the Old Testament prophets had spoken of the day to come when

I will pour out my Spirit upon all flesh,
and your sons and your daughters shall prophesy,
and your young men shall see visions,
and your old men shall dream dreams;
yea, and on my menservants and my maidservants
  in those days
I will pour out my Spirit; and they shall prophesy.   (Acts 2:17, 18)

Not all Christians could prophesy—only the gifted few. Acts speaks of Agabus (11:28; 21:10), Judas and Silas (15:32), the four daughters of Philip (21:9), the prophets and teachers in Antioch (13:1), and the twelve disciples of Ephesus who prophesied immediately after Paul baptized them (19:6). Jesus himself had frequently been called a prophet, of course (Matthew 13:57; Mark 6:4; Luke 4:24; 13:33, 34; John 6:14; 7:40). For the apostle Paul, prophecy was one of God's greatest gifts, as he makes clear in his discussion of tongues and prophecy in 1 Corinthians 14. He seems to define the term to mean intelligible preaching that builds up the church in faith (1 Corinthians 14:6), explains mysteries and conveys knowledge (1 Corinthians 13:2), as opposed to unintelligible tongues-speaking. Much preaching is therefore prophetic, by Paul's definition, even though it might not be prophesying.

Prophets, like apostles, faded in the post-apostolic age. By then the written New Testament was available to guide the church, so official prophets were no longer recognized by the believers. Through their teachers and under the guidance of the Holy Spirit they could discern the will of God from His Word.

Evangelists

In post-New Testament days, this term was generally applied

to the disciples of the apostles, especially those who served as missionaries to Gentiles. In the New Testament the word is used three times: here in Ephesians 4, in Acts 21:8 of Philip, and in 2 Timothy 4:5 of Timothy. Whether the word was a title for a separate office is somewhat doubtful; it actually describes an activity more than an office. An evangelist could be any Christian actively proclaiming (heralding, announcing) that Jesus is Lord and Savior. The term has been used only infrequently throughout church history, and then usually of a person who might have another "official" title, like Timothy, whom Paul exhorts to "do the work of an evangelist," but whose other duties correspond to those of an established pastor.

Pastors and Teachers

Pastor is used only here in the New Testament, but *teacher* is a popular term applied to Jesus 30 times and to church leaders frequently. There were prophets and teachers in Antioch (Acts 13:1); Paul is called a teacher (2 Timothy 1:11). The dangers inherent in teaching are vividly described by James 3:1. Pastors are shepherds, caring for their flocks (see John 21:15-17); teachers share the same responsibility, imparting knowledge as an essential in pastoral care. In the Greek, the form of the phrase "pastors and teachers" indicates that a single person is meant. He is the pastor-teacher, charged with pastoral care and teaching responsibilities in established congregations, as opposed to the apostles, prophets and evangelists who bring new churches into being.

The Living Bible paraphrases Ephesians 4 in a helpful manner, stressing these gifts to the church as activities to be performed rather than as offices to be filled. The one exception is the role of the apostles, who are treated as unique:

> Some of us have been given special ability as apostles; to others he has given the gift of being able to preach well [prophets]; some have special ability in winning people to Christ, helping them to trust him as their Savior [evangelists]; still others have a gift for caring for God's people as a shepherd does his sheep, leading [pastors] and teaching [teachers] them in the ways of God.
>
> Why is it that he gives us these special abilities to do certain things best? It is that God's people will be equipped to do better work for him, building up the church, the body of Christ, to a

position of strength and maturity; until finally we all believe alike about our salvation and about our Savior, God's Son, and all become full-grown in the Lord—yes, to the point of being filled full with Christ (verses 11-13).

Elders

Ephesians 4 says nothing about elders, a title that figures prominently in the later letters. Undoubtedly, in the beginning the apostles were *the* recognized leaders of the church, functioning both in special ways and in ways quite similar to the elders of the Jewish synagogues. Later, the roles of the apostles and elders were so intertwined that the same titles were sometimes applied to one man (the apostle Peter writes, "So I exhort the elders among you, as a fellow elder and a witness of the sufferings of Christ" 1 Peter 5:1). The apostles could be called elders, but in no instance are the later elders called apostles, since they could not have seen the resurrected Lord. Still later, as the apostles grew old and died, other leaders stepped into their vacancies. Many of the functions that had previously been performed by the apostles were then taken over by elders in subsequent generations. These older, respected, proved men became the spiritual leaders of the churches. Quite naturally they were given the familiar title of *elder*. In the Jewish congregations they retained *presbuteros* (elder) as the title; Greek congregations apparently employed the common word for overseer, *episkopos* (bishop). To these men developed the responsibility for oversight, teaching, and modeling the Christian life.

In some very small churches, or in cell groups of larger churches, one man may have served as the elder; in larger groups, several elders jointly served the congregation. They did not view themselves as absolute rulers, for that would be in opposition to Jesus' explicit teaching, but as servants of the church. As servants, they were—

1. To give oversight to all the activities of the church. Oversight involves goal-setting, establishing and evaluating programs, protecting the church from danger of sin (Acts 20:28; 1 Peter 5:1-3).
2. To teach, both formally and informally (Acts 20:28; 1 Timothy 3:2).
3. To shepherd the flock, that is, to provide pastoral care for

133

the spiritual and physical needs of the members (1 Peter 5:2).

4. To lead, which is not the same as to give oversight. Elders are to be out in front, leading the church forward spiritually and evangelistically. If we are right in assuming that the elders succeeded the apostles and prophets in the leadership of the church, then their goal also is to equip the saints "for the work of ministry, for building up the body of Christ . . ." (Ephesians 4).

5. To be a model, an example, for the church (1 Peter 5:3). For this reason the list of qualifications is severe (1 Timothy 3). The church needs leaders whose personal qualities could profitably be imitated. Since the elders are to rule over the church (1 Timothy 5:17; 1 Thessalonians 5:12), it is imperative that they manifest spiritual qualities that will make the Christians want to follow their lead.

A modern parallel will demonstrate this often overlooked role of the eldership. It has been reported that within hours after the first London air raid of World War II, newspaper and radio executives of the city met to determine their role in helping the cause of Britain. They decided they would appeal to their fellow citizens' finest instincts by reporting, whenever possible, examples of courage and heroism. They began with the next air raid. In writing about it later one who was at the meeting declared, "It was established then and there how the people of London would behave while under attack." In like manner the church holds up as models persons of courage and character so that all Christians will know how to behave.

Jewish synagogues employed full-time teachers, supported by the congregation. The early church imitated this pattern, at first supporting the apostles, later supporting some of the elders who worked as pastor-teachers. They labored primarily on behalf of the believers, helping them to gain richer insights into the meaning of their faith and its implications for their conduct. "Let the elders who rule well be considered worthy of double honor," Paul writes to Timothy, "especially those who labor in preaching and teaching" (1 Timothy 5:17). Then he exhorts Timothy to be certain that ruling elders receive the wages such laborers deserve. He writes similarly in Galatians 6:6. "Let him who is taught the word share all good things with him who teaches." In these ruling elders or pastor-teachers is found the prototype of today's full-time ministers.

Deacons

Of deacons there is less to say. If the elders are the older, respected persons (a possible translation for *presbuteros* is grandfather) whose primary responsibilities are oversight, teaching and modeling, then the deacons (servants) are younger men who assist the elders (see Acts 6:1-6) in whatever assignment these leaders give them. They are often elders-in-training. The fact that the list of qualifications for deacons in 1 Timothy 3:8 so nearly parallels those for elders suggests that there may be no clear-cut distinction between their functions. When the assistants to the apostles were appointed in Acts 6 in order to take care of the charitable activities of the church, they very quickly stepped outside the bounds of the brief job description and began preaching the Word (see the activities of Stephen and Philip in Acts 6—8). There seems to be no division between "spiritual" and "physical" activities here. The title of *deacons* implies their readiness to serve at the will of their overseers.

If we are correct in assuming that many of these younger men are elders-in-training, then the elders have an added responsibility—that of preparing the younger men so that they can one day step into the leadership of the church. In the meantime, the elders can work closely with the deacons in the following ways:

1. Study programs. The requirements of today's society demand that church leaders be knowledgeable in several fields. Bible and Christian doctrine head the list of required subjects, including the nature of God, of Christ, of the Holy Spirit, the inspiration of the Scriptures, teachings regarding church, salvation, eternity, etc. In addition, some knowledge of church history is essential, to prevent falling into errors again. Some study of psychology and counseling would be valuable, as would similar studies in missions, evangelism, worship, education, prayer, and so many other subjects.

2. Evangelism. The truly alive church is one that is constantly reaching out to the non-Christians in the community. Elders have had experiences in winning others to Christ; deacons usually have not and would welcome the opportunity to go calling

in order to learn how to lead another person to the Lord.

3. Personal Christian growth. A deacon needs to spend time with an elder to learn how to pray, to tithe, to have a constantly improving Christian home, to develop the fruit of the Spirit (Galatians 5:22, 23) and to assist others in their Christian growth.

4. Teaching. Since elders are to be "apt to teach," each deacon can learn about both formal and informal teaching methods from his elder.

5. Supervision. The oversight task of an elder can best be learned by the deacon as he observes him in action—in elders' meetings, in his work with Bible classes, in his counseling of straying members or his interceding on behalf of an offended one.

6. Long-range planning. The ability to plan for the future and work that plan is not given to everyone. Blessed is the church whose elders frequently look ahead ten or twenty years and then lead the church forward. Blessed is the deacon whose overseeing elder can help him learn to think long thoughts and to see Spirit-filled visions.

The above list has left out the most obvious job of elders in many churches, that of presiding at the Lord's table. The elder will of course want to train his deacon for this assignment, but he will mislead the deacon if he suggests that this is the most important of his duties. In fact, it is not essential to the role of elder at all, any more than passing the offering plate is essential to the role of deacon. We must be careful not to confuse the obvious with the essential.

Leading Through Love

In this short discussion of the church's leaders nothing yet has been said about the one indispensable ingredient in effective leadership. Paul doesn't overlook it:

> Rather, speaking the truth *in love*, we are to grow up . . . into Christ, from whom the whole body . . . makes bodily growth and upbuilds itself *in love* (Ephesians 4:15, 16).

A church, you remember, is unlike any other organization. If it is managed like our government, or a dictatorship, or even an efficient business, it fails as a church. The church's goal is growth, both numerical and spiritual; only love can effect that growth. Without leaders who love their people with the love of Christ, a congregation will ultimately fail. When leaders care more about the prestige of their office than the problems of their people, when they devote themselves to the exercise of power rather than the humility of service, or when they devote their meetings to the maintenance of their property instead of the strengthening of their flock, they are failing to love. Their body cannot then "grow up in every way into him who is the head, into Christ." The highest form of Christian leadership is service in love.

For Further Consideration

1. In what way did Jesus' disciples differ from those of the other religious teachers of His time? Whom do we more closely resemble, His or theirs?
2. *Apostle* has a special meaning in Christian history. What is it?
3. What is a prophet? Why did prophets also fade in the post-apostolic age?
4. Who is an evangelist?
5. Discuss the roles of pastor-teacher and elder. Does your church ask the leaders to fulfill their Biblical assignments?
6. What do deacons do?
7. Why is love indispensable in Christian leadership?
8. Are you satisfied with the way your church is organized and functioning? How would you change it?

CHAPTER FIFTEEN

The Essential Church

(Acts 15)

Just what does a church have to look like in order to be a church? To ask that question is immediately to be reminded again that the church is not a building, but a congregation of people. A church does not have to be a white frame structure with a steeple. But if the church is people, what is essential to their fellowship, so that wherever we go we can recognize a Christian church when we see one?

When visiting India a few years ago, my wife and I had the privilege of worshiping with three congregations on one Sunday. Physically the gatherings were quite dissimilar. The Ennore church was strong, with excellent leadership and a solid, well-maintained building. For the service the women sat on the floor mats on one side of the main room; the benches were reserved for the men, who sat on the opposite side. A few native Indian instruments accompanied the singing. A fairly formal order of worship was observed, led by a highly educated Indian pastor. Later in the morning we visited the Tondiarpet church. Their new building was not a substantial brick and plaster building like the one at Ennore, but one like a large but humble village hut with thatched roof and dirt floor. Mats were used here also, but for both men and women, who again sat on opposite sides of the room. The singing was not accompanied by any instrument, and Communion was served with the common cup (a daring adventure for a foreign visitor). The people were poor and very shy around the American guests.

The third church was the Kilpauk congregation, which met on Sunday mornings at the YMCA but convened in the evenings in the ample living room of the Anglo-Indian minister's home. We felt quite at home with this congregation, sitting on furniture that could have fit into our own American home, with men and women intermingled in the gathering without embarrassment. A piano accompanied the singing and the entire service was in English.

Superficially the three congregations differed markedly from each other in their relative wealth, in language, in relations between the men and women, in the manner of partaking of Communion, in the length and content of the preaching, in their attitudes to the strangers in their midst, in dress—in fact, in just about everything that we observed. And they were different from our congregation in America. Yet in each instance we knew that we were in a Christian assembly. The essentials of the church were there.

Missionary friends describe their worship services. In Ethiopia the Christians meet under a tree for two- or three-hour services. In Brazil simple *bairro* services are held in Christian homes. In Europe formal liturgies prevail, while in Indonesia informal meetings strongly flavored with native customs are the order. Yet all these expressions are called Christian worship and the vividly different members accepted as fully Christian.

To turn from today's varied congregations to the churches of the New Testament is to recognize that variety has colored the church from the beginning. One can hardly imagine two churches more different than the poor but pious church in Jerusalem, barely removed from Judaism in outlook and practice, and the wealthier, wilder church of Corinth, meeting under the shadow of the acropolis where the goddess Aphrodite was maintained by her prostitute-priestesses and where exuberance and sensuality marked and threatened to disrupt the worship of Christ. Yet both are called churches in the New Testament and members of both accepted in the wider Christian fellowship.

Revelation 2 and 3 further illustrates the diversity among the early churches. The church at Smyrna was poor, but Laodicea could boast of its wealth; Sardis had lost its real love for the

Lord, but Pergamum was holding fast to Christ even in the face of persecution.

Such diversity was at once the glory and the predicament of the early church. Christians were instructed by Paul that Christ "has broken down the dividing wall of hostility" between Jew and Gentile, "that he might create in himself one new man in place of the two, so making peace" (Ephesians 2:11-16), but that hard won peace was easier to accept theologically than to live practically. The first major crisis threatening the disunity of the church arose over this issue: Are Jew and Gentile really equal in the church? Can a Gentile become a Christian without also having to fulfill the requirements of the Mosaic law? To be specific, shouldn't he also have to be circumcised, a rite that has been required of every Jewish male from the time of his ancestor Abraham to this day? How can one become a part of God's people unless he fulfills this covenant requirement?

That is the heart of the confrontation recorded in Acts 15 (see also Galatians 2). Paul and Barnabas had returned from their church-planting journey to their home church in Antioch. Upon their arrival they reported their successful activities and the church praised God over the conversion of Gentiles. Not everyone rejoiced, however. Word reached the predominantly Jewish Christian church in Jerusalem about their experiences among non-Jews, and men left Judea for Antioch to correct the impression left by Paul and Barnabas that one could become a Christian without becoming a Jew first. "Unless you are circumcised according to the custom of Moses, you cannot be saved," they insisted. They would not yield on this point; neither would the missionaries. There was only one way to resolve the issue, so the Antioch church quickly moved to dispatch Paul, Barnabas and some others to Jerusalem to counsel with the apostles and elders there. The future of the Christian faith hung in the balance, for if the "Judaizers" were right, Christianity would remain forever a reform sect within the Jewish religion, and nothing more. If Paul and his colleagues were correct, however, people of all races and nations could be welcomed as fellow citizens in the kingdom of God without having to forsake their culture to become circumcised Jews.

The Acts report of the Jerusalem conference (Acts 15) presents a picture of the essential church. It is, in the first place, *an inclusive fellowship*.

You can imagine the shock the Gentile Christians felt when the self-appointed inspectors from Jerusalem told them they could not be saved without being obedient to the customs of Moses. They had never heard such teachings before. They had earlier asked, in one form or another, what they had to do to be saved. From the conversion accounts in Acts we know they had been told they must believe in Christ as Lord and in repentance turn to Him as their Savior. They had been baptized in the name of Christ. They were remaining faithful to the commands of the gospel, meeting regularly with other Christians to study the apostles' teaching, to break bread and pray. Was more required of them?

Yes, the Judaizers insisted. These strict Jewish Christians interpreted the Christian faith as an extension of Judaism, an improvement in some ways because of the coming of the Messiah, but Judaism nevertheless. As blood descendants of Abraham, they had no doubt that only Abraham's lineage could be the people of God, and only through circumcision could those not in his line be adopted as Abraham's heirs. Furthermore, the great lawgiver was Moses, whose laws were from God and had to be obeyed.

While they would have agreed with Paul that we are saved by the grace of God (Ephesians 2:8), they modified His grace by adding the strictures of the law to it. They were not unlike modern modifiers of the gospel who agree that all of us are sinners saved by grace but then add, "However, *unless* you speak in tongues," or "*unless* you repudiate your allegiance to the government," or "*unless* you abandon church buildings and return exclusively to house churches," or "*unless* you give up cosmetics or sex or property or something else," or "*unless* you follow this leader or that leader with his rules and commands . . . you cannot be saved."

Hidden beneath these modifications, which sound respectably religious at first hearing, is the real, altogether quite human, reason. The actual charge is this: Unless you become *like us*, you cannot be saved. Even as great a Christian as Jonathan Edwards, one of the spiritual giants of the eighteenth century, brooded about his salvation in his diary because his experience with Christ did not conform to that expected of him by other religious leaders:

> The chief thing that makes me in any measure question my good estate is my not having experienced conversion in those particular steps wherein the people of New England, and anciently the people of Old England, used to experience it.

He was feeling pressure from others who, however well-meaning, were persuading him that because he was not like them, or had not "experienced" salvation in the same manner as they, he probably was not saved.

A good friend of mine made the same charge regarding my salvation, several years after I had begun my ministry. Because I could not match "experience" stories with him, he sincerely worried about my eternal destiny. He believed in the grace of God, all right, but in the terms of his own experience; he wanted me to become like him.

One of the leaders of the nineteenth-century restoration movement in America felt the same frustration that the Antioch Christians express—and all of us who are not like "them" have felt. Thomas Campbell, who moved to America from Ireland, was an ordained minister of the Old Light Anti-Burgher Seceder Presbyterian Church. The Presbyterian Church was the result of John Knox's reform movement in Scotland. A schism later developed in the Presbyterian Church, and then there were two churches with the dissenters becoming the Seceder Presbyterians. But shortly another schism developed, this one concerning the relationship between civil and ecclesiastical authority. The division was identified by the adjectives Burgher and Anti-Burgher. Then within the Anti-Burgher branch of the Seceder branch of the Presbyterian church yet another schism rent the denomination, this time concerning the power of civil magistrates in religion, so now there were "Old Light Burghers" and "New Light Burghers" as well as "Old Light Anti-Burghers" and "New Light Anti-Burghers." Of course, each splinter asserted itself to be the only true church. What makes the ridiculous even more ludicrous is the fact that the churches in Ireland and America insisted on maintaining these divisions caused by local conditions in Scotland. Beneath each of these schisms lay buried the real issue, which was "Unless you become like me, you cannot be saved." Thomas Campbell and others like him saw through this foolishness and began to appeal for the unity of Christians on the basis of the *essential* New

Testament church. His study of the Scriptures had convinced him that Christ's church was more inclusive of differences of opinion and practice than were the denominations at war with one another in his day. He broke from his denomination to launch a movement of inclusive unity that helped reshape American Christianity in the nineteenth and twentieth centuries.

Campbell's study of the New Testament church led him to his inclusive stance; this was possible, he discovered, because the *church has few essentials*. He learned what the Jerusalem conference concluded. The leaders there found it acceptable to receive uncircumcised Gentiles into the full fellowship of the Christian church because they deduced that faith in Christ does not make the Jewish rite of circumcision an essential part of the conversion process or of church membership. In order to come to that conclusion, the apostles and elders had to distinguish cultural or social requirements from the commands of the gospel.

This is a distinction that Christians still find difficult to make. Mont Smith, Professor of Missions at Pacific Christian College and former missionary in Ethiopia, has devised a Gospel/ Culture Test that he uses to introduce to American Christians the necessity of separating culture from gospel, so that they will not force their foreign missionaries to convert people to American culture rather than to Christ. The missionary "has no right to deculturalize his potential converts as he brings them the gospel," Smith writes. "They do not have to become Americans to become Christians any more than Paul and Barnabas' converts had to become Jews to become Christians." Within the United States, we must be equally alert not to require white-middle-class standards of new Christians who may not be white and middle class.

In his test Dr. Smith lists 56 Scriptural commands or examples and asks church members to mark those with a G that the gospel requires and those with a C that are "commands or practices that reflect a mere practice used perhaps by men or God, but not by command of God." In some cultures or circumstances the command may be valid; in others, not at all. Test yourself on this sample:

1. "Greet one another with a holy kiss . . ." (Romans (16:16).
2. Don't eat meat that has been sacrificed to idols (Acts 15:29).

3. Be baptized (Acts 2:38).
4. "A woman ought to have a veil on her head" (1 Corinthians 11:10).
5. Laying on of hands for ordination (Acts 13:3).
6. "It is indecent for a woman to speak in an assembly" (1 Corinthians 14:35).
7. The first day of the week beginning on Saturday night (Acts 20:7).
8. "I permit no woman to teach men" (1 Timothy 2:12).
9. "Eat what is set before you, asking no questions" (1 Corinthians 10:27).
10. "Are you free from a wife? Do not seek marriage" (1 Corinthians 7:27).
11. Don't eat anything that creeps, or reptiles . . . (Acts 10:12-14).
12. Speaking in tongues (Acts 2).
13. "Wives, be subject to your husbands" (Colossians 3:18).
14. "Work with your hands" (1 Thessalonians 4:11).
15. Eat no man's bread without paying (2 Thessalonians 3:8).
16. If a man will not work, let him not eat (2 Thessalonians 3:10).
17. Urge younger widows to remarry (1 Timothy 5:11-14).
18. Saying "Amen" at end or during prayers (1 Corinthians 14:16).
19. Fasting for spiritual reasons (Matthew 6:17).
20. Selling property when one becomes Christian (Acts 4:37).

As you quickly recognized, some churches have taken strong stands regarding some of these Scriptures. Which ones are essential, however? Smith identifies only two as being gospel commands to be universally applied by the churches.

The key verse in the Acts report of the Jerusalem conference is 15:11: "But we believe that we shall be saved through the grace of the Lord Jesus, just as they will." What is essential to salvation, then, is acceptance of the Lord's freely offered gift of salvation. Peter's gratitude for this grace is implied in the tenth verse: "Now therefore why do you make trial of God by putting a yoke upon the neck of the disciples which neither our fathers nor we have been able to bear?" (v. 10).

James confesses the same sentiment when he appeals to the Jerusalem leaders not to "trouble those of the Gentiles who turn to God." The letter from Jerusalem to Antioch adds, "For it has seemed good to the Holy Spirit and to us to lay upon you *no greater burden than these necessary things*" (v. 28). We shall look at the reason for the "necessary things" in a moment. What is important here is to note the agreement of the Jerusalem conference that only essential requirements should be added. They were content that the Gentiles who had accepted Christ as Lord were their full-fledged brothers and sisters. They were further convinced that the new unity they were enjoying should not be threatened by any unnecessary requirements. Since it is the task of the church to make known what God has done and is doing in the world to break down the barriers between hostile peoples and between human beings and God, nothing that obstructs this God-given purpose can be tolerated.

It is that same conviction that has led generations of unity-seeking Christians to follow the Jerusalem precedent. They seek to be Christians only, allowing no human modification of the New Testament model—either in name or in church practice—to create disharmony.

A tragic illustration of the consequences of "Judaizing" comes from Roland Allen. In his *Spontaneous Expansion of the Church*, he tells of Big Hunter, who was a chief among the Sioux Indians who fled from the United States into Canada to find protection under the Canadian government. Missionaries visited and taught them there, and many accepted the Christian faith, including Big Hunter. But when he told the missionaries that he wanted to become a Christian, he was told that he could—after he had put away all of his wives except one. He did not know how to obey them, because he didn't know how to arrange for the care of his wives. Finally he resolved his dilemma by hanging all but one of them. When he told the missionaries that he had done what they demanded, they drove him away as a murderer. In despair, Big Hunter gave up any hope of becoming a Christian. He married two new wives and finished his days as a heathen.

Were the missionaries wrong? They thought not. Their error, we now know, was that of the Judaizers. They wanted Big Hunter to be saved by the grace of God—and by becoming like them. So convinced were they of the correctness of their position they failed to appreciate that there is no Scripture anywhere that requires a man to be a monogamist in order to be saved! Monogamy is obviously held up as an ideal for Christians (1 Timothy 3) but not as a requirement for salvation. In this case, the missionary's culture took the place of the gospel.

The Jerusalem conference makes it clear that the essential church *transcends all cultural limits*. Christ "has broken down

145

the dividing wall of hostility" (Ephesians 2:14), allowing the church to assume different expressions in different cultures, but holding all Christians together in a bond of peace. Thus the church can flourish all around the globe, adapting itself to suit many cultural requirements, but holding fast to its central commitment to Christ as Lord. It is no accident that many Christian leaders have adopted Meldenius's seventeenth-century slogan, "In essentials unity, in nonessentials liberty, in all things love."

The strong-willed John Wesley could appeal for opinion-transcending oneness in Christ in these words: "I will not quarrel with you about my opinion; only see that your heart is right toward God, that you know and love your neighbor, and walk as your Master walked, and I desire no more. I am sick of opinions; am weary to bear them; my soul loathes this frothy food." Opinions, of course, simply express the biases our culture has fostered in us. The only way to transcend them is through a Lord who is not bound to any culture. Although Jesus was very much a first-century Jew, E. Stanley Jones reminds us that He rose above the limits of His society:

> For there is only one universal Man and only one universal Order. Buddha was Indian, Confucius was Chinese, Moses was Hebrew, Socrates was Greek, Shakespeare was English, Goethe was German, Garibaldi was Italian, Lincoln an American—all were local. Only one transcended the boundaries of race and class and country—only one was the Son of Man.

When the church is kept free of binding cultural entanglements, Christians can then celebrate their freedom and unity. The agenda of the Jerusalem conference contains two items, actually. Item One is the resolution of the question, "What is essential to salvation?" The conference answers by accepting as full members of the church those who have accepted the grace of the Lord Jesus. The many conversion accounts in Acts exhibit the process by which one accepts the free gift of salvation.

The conference does not just answer the question, however. It then moves on to the primary reason for the meeting. It has to resolve another question: *What else must be done for the sake of the church's unity?* Both Jews and Gentiles needed to make some concessions in order for harmony to prevail. The Jewish Christians made the biggest concession in accepting the Gentile

Christians as full members in spite of their differences. They did not impose circumcision or the law of Moses upon the new converts. In conceding on these points, the Jewish Christians were accepting a new definition of the people of God, one which granted the previously intolerable proposition that non-Jews were equally accepted to God through Christ.

Gentile Christians, on the other hand, were asked to honor some specific requests in order to avoid offending their brothers and sisters who held Jewish practices in high regard:

1. "Abstain from the pollutions of idols." Make it clear to all who know you that you share with us a conviction that there can be no other gods but God.
2. "Abstain from unchastity." Our God is holy and He has made His people holy. Let us agree not to sin against God or against persons through sexual misconduct.
3. "Abstain from what is strangled and from blood." Make it possible for us truly to be one and to show our unity by eating together. You know that our Jewish heritage will not allow us to eat meat of an animal that has been strangled, nor can we eat blood. We cannot eat with you if you do these things.

That this last request was a temporary compromise for the sake of unity is evident in the fact that by the second century it is no longer mentioned. The crisis has been averted by the willingness of both parties to express love in these non-essentials.

"Now the Lord is the Spirit, and where the Spirit of the Lord is, there is freedom," the apostle Paul would later write to the Corinthians. The Jerusalem conference has demonstrated that the essential church enjoys the freedom to differ, to grow, to love, and to change as change is required. The essential church is unshackled by tradition, customs and prejudices. It can be inclusive because it requires that the members hold fast to the few essentials that can be observed in any culture while allowing generous freedom in matters not expressly commanded by the gospel. The essential church is jealous to maintain the unity of all believers in Christ.

Let today's church be founded on Christ, pointing to Christ, saving in Christ's name, seeking the lost as Christ sees them.

Let it place no unnecessary burden on the members. Since you cannot demand that everyone in the church agree with you, and since it is impossible for you always to agree with the rest of the members, then unity cannot be found in opinions. Instead, hold fast to what is central to our faith, Jesus Christ, and let everything else be treated as secondary.

We are saved by grace.

We extend grace to one another.

For Further Consideration

1. What other characteristics, besides those discussed in this chapter, *must* the church exhibit to be the church?
2. Why was it so difficult for the Jewish Christians to accept Gentile Christians as equals before God? Do we have any similar difficulties?
3. How inclusive is your church? How open and inviting are you toward persons of a different color, economic status, or educational level?
4. In what ways do we expect other Christians to become like us?
5. Read Dr. Smith's twenty items again. How many of them would you require Christians to practice as essential to the faith? What is the basis of your judgment?
6. Does today's church place any obstacles in the way of evangelism similar to the Judaizers' insistence on circumcision? Do they require that potential converts give up any habits, or adopt a new lifestyle, or make any pledges *before* accepting Christ and being accepted into the body of Christ?
7. What practices in your church derive strictly from our culture and have little to do with the gospel?
8. Why has the church found unity so difficult to attain and maintain?

CHAPTER SIXTEEN

The Future of the Church

The great historian Arnold Toynbee, toward the end of his distinguished career, confessed that his attitude toward religion had reversed itself. He began with a view of religion as the enemy of civilization. Then he saw it as the servant of civilization. In the end, however, he realized that civilization exists for the sake of religion. Society must serve the certain or it flies out of control.

H. G. Wells, never a really religious man, studied the history of the human race and concluded that religion is the first and the last things. Nothing really falls into place apart from God. Perhaps this is what Francis Bacon meant when he said that "a little philosophy inclineth man's mind to atheism; but depth in philosophy bringeth men's minds about to religion." The great nineteenth-century preacher Frederick William Robertson offers this summary of the values that men must not lose:

In the darkest hour through which a human soul can pass, whatever else is doubtful, this at least is certain. If there is no God and no future state, yet, even then, it is better to be generous than selfish, better to be chaste than licentious, better to be true than false, better to be brave than to be a coward. Blessed beyond all earthly blessedness is the man who in the tempestuous darkness of the soul, has dared to hold fast to these venerable landmarks.

But where does one find those landmarks? Where are they upheld, handed down, explained, and justified? In the repository of traditional values, the church.

What are the values that the church can specifically offer the world in the 1980's? Here are a few:

The rule of God on earth. It is not necessary to succumb to the fad of the moment or the tyranny of benighted rulers. The kingdom of God is not only future; it is a present and active force within the humble grasp of every seeker. He who takes his orders from the eternal God is free from the petty regulations of fickle governments.

The person of Jesus Christ. Pundits decry the death of heroes in our time. We have stripped our presidents and every other great person of the last vestige of dignity. But a people without models is a lost people. Without Jesus, the only unscarred person who can lead us out of this moral morass, we are undone. The church offers a broken world an unbreakable leader.

The power of the Holy Spirit. If there is a God who works dynamically for good in this world, then it makes sense for the world to allow His Spirit to have His way. It is good for man to have a God high and lifted up, to worship and adore. It is better also to have a God lowly and caring, to work in and through us for the uplifting of humanity. The church reveres such a God.

The possibility of new birth. To be "born again" was quite popular in the 1970s. Such popularity suggests that the full meaning of this Biblical term has not been comprehended. But the very prevalence of the testimonies to new birth also bespeaks the crying need of sin-soiled men and women to be cleansed and given a chance to start life over again. The church offers that chance.

The church herself. One of the greatest gifts the church can give the world is the gift of herself. Where there is insecurity, she offers stability; where there is anonymity, she offers belonging; where there is rejection, acceptance; where there is exhaustion, regeneration; in place of despair, hope; in place of hatred, love; for superstition, faith; instead of loneliness, family.

A new service. The church exists for others. Those who belong, therefore, now work not for their own salvation, but to rescue others for God. To be Christian is to be servant; in serving one finds his place in God's great scheme of things. This new service leads then to meaning for personal existence.

A longer view. The church is in the world, serving the world, saving the world, for a better tomorrow. The church is in the present, but is anchored firmly in the past, where God was at work, and in the future, where God is preparing an eternal resting place. To be in the church is to be rescued from the cross-currents of competing doctrines, the clever deceits of men, the crafty manipulations of a dehumanizing world. It is to be at home with God, shielded from the poisonous darts of the ruler of this world. It is to be free from anxiety, the plaguing worries of one whose existence is limited to the present.

A unique Book. Everything said in this essay can be found in better form in the Bible. Without these Scriptures Christians would have to join the ranks of the pessimists, for they would have no reason to suspect that tomorrow will be any better than today. With the Biblical record of God's search for man, His efforts to save mankind, and His promises for a brighter future, Christians find themselves optimistically looking forward.

Abraham Lincoln spoke for the modern Christian as well as for himself in his brief comments of appreciation to a delegation of Baltimoreans who presented him a "richly wrought" Bible in the late summer of 1864:

> In regard to this great book, I have but to say, it is the best gift God has given to man. All the good Saviour gave to the world was communicated through this book. But for it we could not know right from wrong. All things most desirable for man's welfare, here and hereafter, are to be found portrayed in it. To you I return my most sincere thanks for the very elegant copy of the great Book of God which you present.

All these values and more the church offers. No wonder that it has stood through the centuries in spite of all the predictions that it would die. In 1816, for example, John Keats offered this valediction of the churches: "They are dying like an outburnt lamp." D. H. Lawrence, another man of letters, wrote in 1924 that the "Christian venture is done." Calling the stature of Christianity a "past greatness," he claimed that by his time the adventure had gone out of Christianity and urged "a new venture toward God." Since 1924, however, the church has claimed new territories, expanded its worldwide membership, and enjoyed its most vigorous missionary period. The church stands.

A Christian Views the Eighties

How then shall we assess the eighties from a Christian perspective? What will happen to our traditional values? Should we be optimistic or pessimistic?

I have already tipped my hand. I look forward to the eighties and the nineties and beyond. This decade will prove an exciting time for Christians. No doubt there is always the very real possibility that the world may blow itself up before the decade is over, or that the Lord will tire of our dallying with His commission, but then, of course, there is still reason for optimism for those whose perspective is not just a world view. Reality is not limited to this time and this section of space; human life does not consist of flesh and blood alone. The message of the New Testament is that the risen Lord has conquered the forces of evil and death. Evil still exists, but so does good, and it is stronger and ultimately victorious.

My optimism stems in part also from the nature of humanity. That we have propensity to sin needs no proof, admittedly, but as we have noted, there is something within us that strains toward the eternal, the true, and the loving. We usually behave like beasts, unfortunately, but we have also shown signs that we want God. Philosophers and theologians—and the plain people that pollsters talk to—agree, in their more sober moments, that life does not, indeed cannot, consist in an abundance of things. Men and women, propped upon every side by their latest purchases, still yearn for normality, and the acceptable norm is not more things but more love, not war but peace, not violence but charity, not selfish paganism but unselfish religion.

The nature of the Christian faith is another reason for hope. There is something both worldly and otherworldly about it. Claiming its origins in Heaven, it stakes out this world as its field of service. It is materialistic enough to appropriate the products of technology for its purposes; it is spiritual enough to warn against making gods of those products. Christianity can live in this world even as it compels us to keep moving toward the next one. Although on the one hand we bemoan the destructive effects of satanic influences turned loose upon us, on the other we see the quiet healing power of the irresistible Spirit at work for God's purposes. There is cause to face tomorrow without anxiety.

The Church in the Eighties

Having asserted that the church will still be around in the eighties, upholding traditional values and providing stability in an unstable world, one final question remains to be answered: How should the church meet her obligations in this decade? Here are several suggestions.

1) *Don't apologize for yourself.* You are older and wiser than many of the young upstarts who threaten to displace you each generation. They have predicted your death, they have scoffed at your fusty, old-fashioned ways, they have condemned you for being irrelevant on the one hand or too modish on the other, and they have even succeeded at times in forcing necessary adjustments upon you. But you have outlived them all. You have no need to be embarrassed because you cannot dance the latest steps or embrace the newest philosophy. You are the church. You do not have to be anything else.

2) *But be the church.* Hang on to your essentials. You exist to call people to the worship of the one true God and to make disciples of the Son. Everything else, no matter how tantalizing, is less important. Discipling involves introducing people to Jesus (evangelism) and helping them to become better acquainted with Him. A congregation that concentrates on worship, evangelism and nurture will find its numbers growing, its spirit deepening, and its world benefiting from its presence.

The modern church can be her best only by returning to her origins. Every period of Christian advance has been preceded by a rediscovery of the essence of the church's mission. E. Stanley Jones says that in the beginning "Pentecost saved the disciples from the trivial, the marginal, the irrelevant." A return to the Pentecostal beginnings, then, can rescue the church of the eighties from a similar danger. Acts 2 emphasizes the prayers of the disciples, the power of the Holy Spirit, the persuasiveness of the preaching, the centrality of faith in Jesus, the closeness of the continuing community that met regularly for prayer, study of the apostles' teaching, the breaking of bread, and fellowship. They loved and took care of one another. They reached beyond their fellowship to share their vibrant faith with others. They did not worry about buildings or budgets or offices or rituals or reputation. They flourished, because they concentrated on the essentials.

It was a call back to the essentials which that famous little old lady made so pointedly in the English cathedral. The guide was waxing eloquent about the beauties of the building, but the impertinent tourist stopped him with her question, "Young man, stop your chattering and tell me, has anyone been saved here lately?" She may have been a bit rude, but at least she understood that the church was not called to congratulate herself on aesthetic achievements, but to lose herself in her rescue mission.

3) *Love your people.* Jesus' description of His people has never changed: "By this all men will know that you are my disciples, if you have love for one another" (John 13:35). The church will have many programs, of course, but the human tendency to force people to serve programs must be stifled. A church that preaches the importance of the family, for example, must not then segregate and frustrate families through programs that invariably divide them into age categories or demand they spend most of their time "at church!"

Let the church be organized for the sake of people. Let her not become merely another social organization, offering a routine cup of coffee to troubled men and women seeking meaning for their lives. Let the ministers speak boldly to the human situation, even if their words are unpopular. Ronald Osborn's quip that the "prophet who feeds on locusts and wild honey can afford to make enemies; the Levite with a $1 million temple to pay for is concerned to make friends" is not beside the point. A church majoring in building construction is not majoring in people; a church imitating the social clubs that abound in every community is not majoring in people's deepest needs. It is appropriate for every congregation to ask at the threshold of a new decade, "Has anyone been saved here lately?" If not, why not?

4) *Be ye therefore holy—but not aloof.* Here's the most difficult challenge congregations face. Jesus instructed His disciples to be a city set upon a hill, a light placed upon a stand. The church therefore is called to be above, separate, a shining example in a dark world. That's holy—but it is also aloof. And Jesus called upon His disciples to be the salt of the earth, which is no good until it is mingled with what it is to preserve and penetrate. So the church has to do double duty. She must almost contradict herself to be true to herself. She is to be holy, separated from the immorality and temptations of the world; she is also to be involved, rolling up her sleeves and soiling her clothes in self-

less labor on behalf of those who need her most.

Jesus calls for Christians who are assured of their personal relationship with God, not hugging their personal salvation to themselves but energetically concerned to do battle with the evils of this world for the sake of others.

Wouldn't it be an exciting decade if the church once again had to plead guilty to the charge Julian the Apostate in the fourth century leveled at Christians? He accused them of trying to gain converts by bribing the sick: "These impious Galileans give themselves to this kind of humanity; as men allure children with a cake, so they . . . bring converts to their impiety. . . . Now we can see what it is that makes these Christians such powerful enemies of our gods. It is the brotherly love which they manifest towards strangers and towards the sick and the poor."

That's quite a compliment, to be accused of practicing brotherly love!

5) *Think big thoughts.* A dying church embroils itself in petty arguments, in adherence to small principles, in picky attention to details perpetuating a past glory. The challenges of the 80's are too grave for the church to indulge in disputes about clothes or hair length or changing canons of social taste. She must not be deflected from the larger issues of mercy and justice and love in the gospel. She dare not congratulate herself on yet another balanced budget when a world is crying for her to move out in faith. She must be too big to be drawn into disputes with other Christians who differ somewhat on minor doctrinal matters. There is, after all, "one body and one Spirit . . . one hope . . . one Lord, one faith, one baptism, one God and Father of us all." The unity of the church can be achieved only by thinking large thoughts and pursuing large goals.

6) *Simplify.* We marvel over the great European cathedrals that medieval Christians built to the glory of God, but we quickly admit that the challenge of the 80's cannot be met by building more elegant sanctuaries. In the face of threatening world famine, with the desperate plight of the earth's teeming refugees, with the specter of war shadowing the globe, Christians cannot amuse themselves with accumulating more and more material splendor at home and at church. A simpler corporate and personal lifestyle is demanded. Sharing is the byword of the ·80's. The magnificent structures of medieval

Christianity were matched by the dazzling wealth of the decorated clergy—and the relative poverty of the believers. The more democratic 80's demand a more democratic church. No monarch-ministers are called for; a servant church must have many servants, and they shall be called fellow ministers. The priesthood of all believers remains the unfulfilled promise of the Protestant reformation. Simple church structures, simplified organization, simple lifestyles, and shared possessions and responsibilities, will mark the serving church in this decade.

7) *Be adaptable.* Hold to the essentials, but in everything, be willing to adjust. Mainline denominations have lost their ability to adapt to quickly changing times. Encrusted with traditions and complicated organizational structures, they testify to a *former* dynamic. They are on the defensive, peering from behind their fortress walls at an encroaching army of radical Christians who care neither for their splendor nor their respectability. The earliest churches had neither buildings nor reputation, but firmly grasping a few essentials of the faith they adapted themselves variously to make their assault on a world gone to the devil. It was only later that their success forced them to institutionalize, in order to preserve their gains. Then they lost their forward momentum.

In the 80's the church has a superb opportunity to evaluate and change. The Sunday school, for instance, is now 200 years old. It has served well, but the time may have come for this educational tool to take on a new appearance. House churches, small Bible studies, weekend retreats, college-level Bible courses and other expressions are now emerging and may change the traditional Sunday school dramatically. Revival meetings, which were so successful in past generations, are largely dying out, being replaced by person-to-person evangelism. The multiplying audiovisual tools offer a host of new ways to teach old truths.

In these and other matters, serving churches will ruthlessly examine their practices to find ways to adapt to a changing society's changing needs. The morning worship service may not continue to begin at eleven o'clock. And the sermon may move from the pulpit to the round table. Nineteenth-century practices will give way to twentieth-century realities.

8) *Be faithful unto death.* In the midst of the changes, however, the essentials will be preserved, the truthful traditions main-

tained. Centered on the gospel of Jesus Christ, the church will be

steadfast, immovable, always abounding in the work of the Lord, knowing that in the Lord [her] labor is not in vain.

also by LeRoy Lawson . . .

The New Testament Church/then and now (Workbook)
Closely correlated with the author's exciting text. Helps both beginning and advanced students dig deeper into the meaning and work of the New Testament Church, and to find their own place in it (88586).

The Lord of Parables
Here you'll meet the Lord himself and be taught by Him. You'll find He's spreading His banquet table for *you*. Renew your acquaintance with these parables and with the *Lord of Parables*. Available January 1984 (Instructor, 39980; Student, 39981).

The Lord of Promises
"For persons who would like to learn the secret of living an extraordinary life." If *you* would, Jesus makes you some incredible offers . . . (Instructor, 39988; Student, 39989).

The Lord of Possibilities
"To study Christ's miracles is to enter with awe into a world in which God is in charge. . . . This is a study of faith—*our* faith" (Instructor, 39994; Student, 39995).

The Family of God
What does it mean to become involved with the work of the church and with other believers? This book answers some of the more difficult questions that bother new and prospective Christians (39970).

Up From Chaos
Man has come a long way since God said, "Let there be light." But which way? This book demonstrates the relevance of Genesis for today (40070).

Available at your Christian bookstore or

TEXTBOOKS

**Christian Doctrine: "The Faith . . .
Once Delivered"**
edited by William J. Richardson
   Eighteen essays on the main doctrines of the Christian
faith as they relate to the confession, "Jesus Christ is
Lord." An inspirational volume for church leaders on
understanding and communicating their faith (88588).

The Church On Purpose
by Joe S. Ellis
   A valuable resource for the local church leader. Helps
leaders identify the areas where change is needed and
suggests ways for bringing it about (88584).

Introduction to Christian Education
by Daniel, Wade, and Gresham
   "Could be the best available on the subject" (*Christianity Today*). Up-to-date information on practical teaching methods; extensive treatment of age characteristics,
curriculum, administration, and para-church organizations (88581).

The Christian Minister
by Sam E. Stone
   A practical approach to the preaching ministry; much
specific direction on the minister's work—preaching,
calling, keeping records, managing time (88580).

Ministering to Youth
edited by David Roadcup
   Prepares the youth minister for beginning a ministry
with youth in the local church. The emphasis on effective
ministry is on discipling youth through Bible study,
fellowship, and opportunities for service (88582).

Available at your Christian bookstore or

STANDARD PUBLISHING